Why Normal Isn't Healthy

How to Find Heart, Meaning, Passion, and Humor on the Road Most Traveled

Bowen F. White, M.D.

◧ HAZELDEN®

INFORMATION & EDUCATIONAL SERVICES

TRANSITIONS
BOOKPLACE

Hazelden

Center City, Minnesota 55012-0176

1-800-328-9000

1-651-213-4590 (Fax)

www.hazelden.org

ISBN: 1-56838-559-5

Library of Congress Cataloging-in-Publication Data

[to come]

04 03 02 01 00 6 5 4 3 2 1

Cover design by

Interior design by

Typesetting by

Why Normal Isn't Healthy

Dedication

[to come]

Contents

Foreword

[to come]

Acknowledgments

[to come]

Letter to the Reader

[to come]

INTRODUCTION

I was born dependent. Taught to be codependent. Worked hard. Learned to compete. Focused on self-improvement. Learned to live my life being who other people wanted me to be. And I can die without ever knowing who I am. That may be normal, *but it certainly isn't* healthy.

versus

I was born dependent. Taught to be co-dependent. Learned self-acceptance. Learned that I am the person I was conditioned to be. Began to change myself. Played more. Grew to be the person I was inspired to become. And will die knowing that in some small way the world is a better place because I was born. That may not be normal, *but it* is *healthy.*

Long ago our ancestors lived as hunter-gatherers. Before we domesticated plants and animals, before we came together in cities, the seeds of culture sprouted out of the hunter-gatherer psyche. Those first sprouts grew, flowered, and had progeny. Our current cultural norms are the product of that which began long ago. And in the context of that developmental process, those norms are logical. They make exquisite sense but that doesn't mean they are healthy.

One way to think about this developmental process, this evolutionary process, is as a movie that began with the appearance of *Homo sapiens*, human beings. If we could watch that movie from then to the present, we could follow the progress of humanity and see why people are the way they are. We could see that physically we haven't changed that much from our ancestors. But culturally, the differences are dramatic yet logical in the context of the movie. They are "dramatic" in the sense that they've changed significantly and that they are so diverse globally. The differences are the necessary result of people living over time in a particular environment.

Cultural evolution over thousands of years has given us the diversity now evident as we begin the twenty-first century. And each of us carries our local culture like a baton. We pass the baton from generation to generation, parent to child, teacher to pupil, and so on. Mostly, we do so without thinking. We simply do what we learned to do in our local environs on the road to becoming a grownup. We do what was appropriate as modeled by others. And we turned out all right didn't we? Of course we did. But while "all right," may be normal, it is not the same as healthy.

We cannot run the movie backward. What a shame. For if we could rewind the film and watch as it replayed the movie, our differences, while abundantly clear, would be exquisitely logical. And with that logic we could better understand our differences and each other. But that movie does not exist.

But we can, through the mind's eye, examine what we have been handed by previous generations. We can see both the healthy and the normal, but not so healthy, deposits previous generations have made into our individual psyches. We can then explore the implications for our relationships, all our relationships, individual and collective.

We can choose what is healthy and keep what we choose. What we then pass on can be done with awareness. In choosing to pass along only what is healthy, and to be healthy ourselves, we push our local culture toward a healthier norm.

If that movie existed then all of us would be able to understand why people act the way they do in a given circumstance. Our differences would no longer be a source of judgmental thinking. Rather, we would be curious to see how other members of the human family lived their lives, handled their responsibilities, worked, and played. And, as we viewed those activities we would learn from their performance. Encounters with difference inform.

Our focus here, however, will be on those things we share in common regardless of our differences, for we share much more in common than we share in differences. When I say "we" the reference is to the collective we of the industrialized world. For there may still be a few places left that haven't been contaminated by an industrialized culture. They have survived insulated from the pressures of the contemporary, digital, global marketed, multitasking, rest of us. This book is not for them.

I used to be normal. Still can be. But, I have made some progress. There are periods when I am remarkably healthy. More than there used to be. Not as often as there will be. I'm a work in process: step ahead, make progress; step back, make progress. There is progress. It just isn't always forward.

What I see initially as a step backward may turn out to be a step out of harms way, like stepping back on the curb just before the bus zips by. Or a step forward may be into an emotional abyss, a free fall into some psychic pain that forces unwanted but needed learning. It's all grist for the evolutionary mill. I am in a developmental process, an evolutionary process, the starts and stops of which all serve the unfolding of my human potential, which ultimately folds into humanity's potential.

The individual atom of the cultural structure is a single person. And individual humans bonded together in family systems comprise cultural molecules. Those family systems joined in local communities form larger cultural structures, and so on.

There are great differences between cultural clusters. Those differences provide a delightful variety in the bouquet of our larger human family. That variety provides color that allows us to see those differences more clearly because of the obvious contrast to our own local experience. And we can note those differences, appreciate and learn from them. It is often through the experience of difference that we learn.

But, again, this book is not about learning from our differences. Rather, it is about exploring the things we share in common regardless of our differences. The irony is, by exploring what we share in common, we can better understand our differences. Armed with that understanding, our differences are less likely to become a distraction in our efforts to learn what we can from each other and to make our blue oasis in space a safer place for all cultures to thrive.

If you ask someone to free-associate with the concept of evolution and natural selection, they very well might say, "survival of the fittest." And if you then asked them to say what that means, they might say: "Because of limited resources there is competition for those resources and only the fittest survive. Competition weans out the weak. Only the strong survive to replicate and pass on their genes." So it is through competition that life evolves.

Let's take another, more long-term view. Survivability is diminished if we continue to destroy others as we compete for limited resources. Why? The tools now available to us to defeat our competitors are both horrific and indiscriminate. Not only are we capable of eliminating the competition, we are capable of eliminating life as we know it, period. Obviously, that is counter to survival.

Besides, evolution really has to do with variation and adaptation. Stephen Gould in the *Mismeasure of Man*, writes, "Evolution occurs by the conversion of variation within populations into differences between populations." He goes on to say, "*Natural selection works by differentially preserving the variation that confers better adaptation in changing local environments.*" And finally, "variation within a population . . . becomes converted into differences through time . . . "

So we have evolved to the place where our own evolution becomes instructive and recognize that our animal sensibilities must be subordinated to our human intellect and highest values. War as a tool for conflict resolution represents an insane take on the "survival of the fittest" notion. We must select out a variation from this old norm that allows for better adaptation to our current global environment. "Think global, act local" takes on a new connotation.

Everything is connected to everything else. We have seen the Earth from space. We are all in this together and we recognize the necessary value of collaboration. Our survival depends upon it. We are one human family. Every member adds value. Although, we often question what value we add. That's part of normal not being healthy. And every member lost diminishes us all. The poet, John Donne, said it best:

"No man is an island, entire of itself; every man is a piece of the Continent, a part of the main; if a clod be washed away by the sea, Europe is the less, as well as if a promontory were, as well as if a manor of thy friends or of thine own were; any man's death diminishes me, because I am involved in Mankind; And therefore never send to know for whom the bell tolls; it tolls for thee."

"No man is an island," we are all connected together. Therefore, one thing we can all do to serve the common good is to be healthy ourselves. That is what this journey is about. And the definition of health I'll use is from Ashley Montagu. He said that health "is the ability to love, to work, to play, and to think soundly."

Onward toward health.

CHAPTER 1

THE FOURTH POLE

We are going to take a journey together, you and I. You won't find our destination on a map. But it is a terrain that some people have traveled regardless of where they have been. Where we are going cannot be reached by car. But all roads lead there. There is no train to board to travel these tracks. But, all tracks lead there. There is no plane to take to get where we are going. But all flight ends there. There is no ship that sails into these waters. Yet, all ships dock there. Going by foot will not get us there. But, wherever we walk we end up there. The Internet cannot reach this place for it cannot be found in cyberspace.

We are going to the Fourth Pole.

There may be some confusion in your mind for our schooling did not include this pole with the others. We grew up learning about the North Pole and the South Pole. In fact, that was all we studied. The Third Pole was neglected too. And, if studied, was not so named. For it is the highest place on Earth, Mount Everest. In light of the above, one might think that the Fourth Pole would be the lowest spot on the planet. One might think that it is the opposite of the Third Pole and therefore think it the deepest place in the ocean or the center of the Earth. But that would not be the case. It is the center, all right, but not of the planet. It is the center, the deepest place in the human psyche. It is the place that Rumi referred to in his poem:

Keep walking, though there's no place to get to

Don't try to see through the distances

That's not for human beings

Move within, but not the way fear makes you move

Go to the well

Move as the Earth and moon move

Circling what they love

Whatever circles comes from the center.

The center is our destination. "Move within" indeed. We are going to the center where we all live, regardless of where we live. We are going past our differences to the heart of our essential nature. We are going on a journey to the center of the millennial human.

And, although we travel together, we travel alone. It is a paradox. Why? Why not! After all, we are a paradox. We are there wherever we go. There is no there where we are not. There is no there there. While the other poles are inaccessible and only rarely visited, the Fourth Pole is accessible to each of us but also entered only rarely. Why? Because normal isn't healthy. When we think of adventure we think of the outward journey like Admiral Perry to the North Pole or Edmund Hillary to the top of Everest. The adventure here is inward. No travel is required. Your passport is your intention.

Why should we go there? Because "it's there"? No, because we are there. And to be fully us, to complete our understanding of our house of selves, our center is the core substance that the rest of us circles. To not know it, is to not know ourselves. Socrates said it: "know thyself." That is our task here, to know ourselves. Hence, the center is the goal.

All our orbital activities spring out of that center; "whatever circles comes from the center." And it is at the center that we are all connected. Paradox again.

When we know ourselves at the center, we know who is inside everyone else. And that connection allows our differences to be seen in perspective, i.e., different expressions of our common humanity and common beauty. No one is more significant, more important than the next. Yet all are significant and important. But, because normal isn't healthy, we often feel neither. Why? Stick around. That's what our journey will reveal.

Rumi's poem talks about going within, "but not the way fear makes you move." Interesting caveat... fear is the driver of the stress response. And the stress response is a survival response. Why does Rumi admonish us to move within fearlessly? Could it be that moving within driven by fear will only allow us to focus on the survivability of our circumstances. If our only concern is survival, our expectations are too low. Survival is important, but it is not enough. Life is a terminal condition. What does that say about survival? Besides, we can survive our whole lives and never live them.

But, survival is a beginning, and we are at the beginning. So, let's start there. In this new millennium there is an appreciation of the ever-increasing pace of human endeavor. The rapidity of change that has become the norm is spoken and written about daily. It's as if the velocity of history is increasing and pulling us along in its slip stream. If we don't move with the times, we will be left behind. And all indications are that the quick step, power walk of life will not slow any time soon. Quite the opposite.

Just as we heard from the Hollywood version of a Wall Street deal doer that "greed is good," speed is good is the order of the day. Faster and faster computers allow faster and faster transactions. Rapid cycle time allows deliverables to appear at the customer's door soon after ordering. Twenty-four by seven service, trading, ordering, and complaining allows us to do more in the time we have. And more is better, right? Good question. What do you think?

Because normal isn't healthy ,the cultural norm is a resounding YES. Speed is good and more is better. So, we want more, faster. Gee, fits nicely with greed is good. No wonder we have so much trouble knowing what is enough. *The Wall Street Journal* recently had a front page story about the "haves" wanting more. Is "enough," in fact, an antiquarian concept? Better question. What do you think?

But here, right now, let's slow down a bit. For a brief few moments let us punch out from the hurry of the work-a-day world. Let us stop contracting our words and our lives to cram more in faster. Then, perhaps we can see some options that might be healthy but not normal. Are you with me on this? I know it is a whacky idea but hey, we can punch back in whenever we choose.

"Halt, who goes there?" says the guard at the treasure house door. Slowing everything down, better yet, stopping to reflect on our situation allows for some introspection. I know that it may feel awkward to be introspecting when you could be prospecting for clients or doing some other important grownup activity on the road to building wealth. But, we are the object of inquiry here. It is hard to hit a moving target. To make an investigation into our center we have to "halt" to investigate the "who."

Anthony de Mello in *One Minute Wisdom* tells the following story:

'When a disciple came from a far away country, the Master asked,"What are you seeking?"

"Enlightenment."

"You have your own treasure house. Why search outside?"

"Where is my treasure house?"

"This seeking that has come upon you."

At that moment the disciple was enlightened. Years later he would say to his friends, "Open your own treasure house and enjoy your treasures."

Because normal is not healthy, we look outside for the treasure. Sometimes we refuse to halt and look inside our own treasure house until we develop an illness or experience some other world-stopping event. Then as a result, we have the time to reflect. However, we may not use that time productively. In the sick role we have permission to let go of most of our important grownup responsibilities and get well. But what we often do is obsess about something that we should be doing. When we cannot "do" we feel non-productive. It is "down time." So we obsess.

Why wait for a world-stopping event to examine our lives? Indeed, that is exactly the point. The Fourth Pole awaits any of us willing to accept the challenge and go down. Its location requires going down into our interior.

But this "down time" is productive. When we "Go to the well," to our own deep waters, we invest in our own well-being. It is wealth building in the truest sense, for wealth originally meant well- being.

CHAPTER TWO

REALITY IS THE LEADING CAUSE OF STRESS

"Reality is the leading cause of stress. I can take it in small doses but as a lifestyle I found it too confining. It expected me, to be there for it all the time and well, with all I have to do, I had to let something go. Now, since I put reality on the back burner, my days are jam packed and fun filled."

This quote is from Jane Waggoner's delightful book, *Search For Signs of Intelligent Life in the Universe*. It is spoken by a bag lady in New York City, the character Lilly Tomlin made famous in her one-woman show. Buttons with the, "Reality is the leading cause of stress" line are popular because everyone can relate. We can also relate to "my days are jam packed" in last line above. But we have a little problem with experiencing them as "fun filled."

Do we have to "put reality on the back burner" to have fun? That's what it seems like. After all, with all the problems in the world and all the stress in our lives, escaping reality seems to be required. But, just as the cold hard reality of the ancestral world put evolutionary pressure to work creating Homo sapiens, our current life circumstance is putting pressure on us to experiment and discover the variation that allows us to better adapt. The adjustments we make may serve our own personal evolution. What we may discover may help us to see that stress is really the spice of life and that we can have a few more laughs and a little more fun along to way. That wouldn't be normal but it would be healthy.

LIFE IS STRESSFUL, THEN WE DIE

Stress is a word we hear and talk about all the time, so it's a good place to start. The easiest way for me to jump into this is to just have you free associate with the word stress. Think about stress, and whatever you think about as you free-associate; whatever comes up for you, write down. Go ahead. I'll wait. Here's a sample list from a group with whom I recently met:

Other people.

Humanity.

I'm okay you're not.

Loss of control.

Close down.

Anxiety.

The weather.

Lack of balance.

Exhaustion.

Sleeplessness.

Adrenaline.

Expectations.

Perfectionism.

Not enough time.

Not enough money.

Traffic.

Jobs.

Technology.

Guilt.

Shame.

Relationships.

Marriage.

Prior marriage.

Family.

Children.

Neighbors.

Co-workers.

Sobriety.

Age.

[graphic] Now we're going to do a little systems thinking. Here we have a closed loop system. There's going to be INput and output in this system. And if you think about a systems approach to the problem of stress, a couple of things immediately stand out. One: There are stressors. These are the INputs that we feel are causal. When you're anxious there's usually some cause for the anxiety. Often it has to do with other people, relationships. We have relationships at work and at home. So a lot of what stresses us is connected to relationships. Therefore, a lot of what we're going to be talking about is relationships.

You've heard of the feather effect? Let's say a whole bunch of things have gone wrong in your day. Then your kid does something, and you go ballistic. It's the feather. It's not what your kid did that caused you to de- compensate. It's everything else that you're carrying around and stuffing, maybe work, and other things, traffic. You get home and your child puts the feather on the pile. You just explode.

So we have stress at home, stress at work, stress in traffic. Stressors wherever we turn. And if our home life is stressful and our work life is stressful, and it's stressful going back and forth, would it be fair to say that life is stressful? Yes. Is life fair? No. Is it going to get fair? No. Life is stressful and then we die.

That's an uplifting thought. And who knows, death may be stressful. Even in the best-case scenario, I think it's going to be stressful for me. I think you can view life as a movie and when we die we go over our movie with God. I don't know about you, but that will be a little stressful for me. I'm counting on a Divine sense of humor.

And because life isn't fair, I think we have the right to whine, bitch, complain, and moan. Maybe even get that little blood vessel at the temple to pulsate. I think we should take five minutes out of every day to really get into it, but at the end of five minutes, now what? That life is unfair is a given. That being true, what are we going to do now that our five minutes are up? Indeed.

We have stressors. We have life stressing us, and if we took all of the stressors: home life, work life, traffic and put them in this box with an x on it, we have life putting certain things into our INbox. And then we respond to life by what goes out of our OUTbox. The common responses that we generate when life stresses us are more negative than positve.

So we have life putting certain things into our INbox and then often our responses are more negative than positive. So, it is possible for us to respond negatively to our lives. Would all the negative people out there please stand up? I certainly don't see myself as a negative person but I know well how to make a bad situation worse. I know how to compound a problem by virtue of my response to the problem. Why would we respond negatively in our home life or our work life? We're not negative people, at least most of us.

Think about this. When you were a little kid and you stressed the grownups, how did you see them respond? Anger, frustration, yelling...negatively. If it was snowing out and they had to drive you someplace, it had a negative charge. It was a bad thing. " If you had to drive in this, you'd be unhappy too!" Our conditioned database of life responses comes out of early training. In a sense, we're doing what we know. The baton has been passed and now we are them. We are the people we used to complain about. We are the grownups and we can be doing what is normal but not healthy. But, it is what we learned.

I think the control piece is a big one. Any time you think about stress you want to focus energy and attention where you have power and control. Energy follows attention and what you pay attention to you have energy for. Where do we tend to focus here in this closed loop system? We focus on what is coming at us from the environment. We focus on INput, other people.

We have other people putting things into our INbox. The tendency is to focus on what's coming at us and to allow that to drive behavior and mood. And how do we end up feeling?

Negative. Stressed.

How much control do you have over what your ex puts into your INbox? Your spouse puts into your INbox? You kids put into your INbox? Your co-workers put into your INbox. The other drivers on the highway—how much control do you have over INput in this system?

Some of you may feel that you have quite a bit of control over what life places into your INbox. Others may feel quite the opposite, that they have very little control over INput. I would side with the latter group.

Now I said control and not influence. And the reason I make the distinction is that in dealing with stress, it's important to focus your energy and attention where you have power and control. And my bias is that we don't have control over what life puts into our INbox. We don't have control over how other people treat us. You don't have control over the deadline your boss gives you. You don't have control over someone calling in sick the day before the deadline is due. You don't have control over whether or not your parents get divorced. You don't have control over your selection in the IRS audit lottery.

So the flashlight of our attention is on what is coming at us from the environment, on what life is putting into our INbox. And our energy system is driven by what we pay attention to. So, we have energy to deal with the behavior of these other people. But they're driving how we use our energy.

Here's the kicker. Like other animals, we have been conditioned by what has come at us from the environment in the past. We developed a set of behaviors in response to certain stimuli. We operate out of that conditioned database of responses. In fact, other people may actually know something about that learning. They may know how we're going to respond and therefore know what to put into our INbox to get us to do some predictable behavior. And they use our predictability to manipulate us. The problem is, sometimes it works.

I think most of our human relationships are about trying to figure out what to put into someone else's INbox to get them to do something, or to feel something. It isn't just that other people do that to us. We do that to others. It's a good example of normal not being healthy. It consumes a great deal of energy trying to figure out how to get people to do things. But, sometimes it works. So, we do what we learned, just like little children.

Imagine this scenario. Kids get together in the neighborhood to figure out some kid scam. The big kids are huddled together working on the plan. One of the planner's little sister is listening in to the conversation and hears her big sis say, "but, first we'll have to ask mom permission." The younger sibling knows that it's her mom too, so she runs in mom's direction. Her big sister sees her and runs after her. "What the heck do you think you're doing?"

"Well, you said we had to get mom's permission first. So, I was gonna ask…"

"You dummy. You can't just ask her out of the blue. You have to wait 'til she's in a good mood."

Good mooooooooooooooooooooooooood.

Timing is everything. Ever try to milk a cow at noon? You can milk them in the morning, and you can milk them in the evening. Forget noon. Timing is everything. And we learned when to milk our parents. Wait until they're in a good mood then, attack. And, guess what happens? It works. So, we do what we know works. We do what we learned and what is familiar to us. But just because something works doesn't mean it's a good idea.

It's not the best way to have healthy relationships because our energy is spent trying to manipulate other people. And when other folks call us on it, our response is denial. "How dare you say I'm a manipulative person. I am not like that. I can't stand manipulative people." Truth is, that's what we learned. It's normal but not healthy.

Because of our ability to manipulate others, we get control and influence mixed up. They are not the same thing. We do have influence over others and control over ourselves. Part of normal not being healthy is that we think that we should have control where we don't.

Say the person you are going with or married to is depressed. How does it feel being around them? Depressing. There may be a part of you that tries to figure out what the right combination of words are in the right order to place into their INbox to get them to feel better. You try several things and fail. There may be some part of you that thinks, *I were just more clever, smarter, or something, I could figure out that right combination of words.* The fact is, another's mood is not your responsibility. Your own mood is your responsibility. But, we give power and control over to others and allow them to drive our mood. So, now your melancholy is their fault. Tell me, is that healthy?

By the way, what happens when someone figures out that we are trying to manipulate them into doing or feeling something? This is interesting. Think of your classic stereotypic salesperson. What puts you off as you consider the stereotype? Could it be that we feel a sense of pressure from them to do what they want us to do? Once we can sense that pressure, it creates resistance in us.

The relationship between control and motivation is inverse. The more controlling we are of others, the more resistance we create to the very thing we want them to do. The more controlling we are of others, the more we demotivate them to change. If high control worked to get people to change, our prison system would work---high control, little positive change.

We do have control in this closed loop system. Although we do not have control over what life puts into our INbox, we do have control over how we

19

respond to INput. If we focus on what goes out of our OUTbox, we attend to the place in the system where we have power and control. Here, a perceptual shift, from INput to OUTput, brings with it a responsibility shift. Before, other people were the problem in my life. Now, I see that I am the problem in my life. I am THE problem. But, I am also the solution.

Without anyone else changing, without anyone else doing anything differently, what are the things I can do to be healthy: have a healthier relationship with myself, healthier relationships with other people, be more effective at whatever I do, and have more fun getting better. Those are things that interest me. Remember, health here is concerned with our working, loving, playing and thinking.

By seeing myself as the problem in my life, it doesn't mean that other people aren't stressors. But, when they are THE problem, then I focus attention and energy on trying to control them to change. I consume vast amounts of energy and get a poor return on my energy investment. If I focus on motivating myself to change, I get a much better return on my energy expenditures.

The discomfort I feel when I am stressed and responding in a negative mode, can be instructive. At my best, I want to use the discomfort that I feel as a signal that I need to change. Without any of the familiar stressors of my life changing, I want to start responding in healthier ways. It won't be easy. If someone says it's easy, it's an infomercial. It's easier to continue to play the role of the victim. But that's an unempowered role. And, it's an illness trap.

But avoiding stress related illness is only a start. It's a good start. Ultimately, however, the goal is to use the unfairness of life, the stressors on the journey, as a stimulus to growth and emotional maturity.

CHAPTER 3

OF MICE, rather rats, AND MEN

Let's see how being a victim ties back in with normal not being healthy. What we're going to do is a little rat science. We're going to take two genetically identical rats and put them in identical cages. We're going to shock both rats simultaneously with the same amount of current. Let's call them Rat # 1 and Rat # 2.

Both rats have wires around their tails. Those wires will be the vehicles to shock them both at random for three weeks. But Rat #1 has a bar in his cage connected to the electrical device. So when he gets the shock in his INbox he can push the bar and it turns off the shock. Rat # 2 has the same kind of bar in his cage, but it is not hooked up to the electrical device. So it doesn't matter what he does because it doesn't make any difference.

We're going to shock the rats at random for three weeks. Rat #1 can turn off the shock for himself, and here's the caveat—when he turns off the shock for himself, he turns off the shock for Rat #2 simultaneously. It doesn't matter what Rat #2 does, it doesn't make any difference. He has to wait for his empowered sibling to turn off the shock.

There is no pattern to the shocks delivered to the rats. Imagine what it's like for Rat #2. Hanging out in his cage, sleeping and eating. He gets this bolt of electricity into his INbox. What's his first response? If you get shocked, what do you do? You remove yourself from the painful stimulus. You want to get away.

So he pulls a geographic displacement. He moves to another part of the cage, right? Now is it safe over there?

No. Why?

Because the wire is hooked up to his tail. Wherever he goes, it goes with him. So he goes over to where he thinks it's safe and he gets shocked again. It's like someone in a bad relationship. She gets shocked, metaphorically, and says, "I'm getting out of here." Then she gets in a different relationship. "Damn, it's the same person with a different name. I thought I left you behind."

If the other person is the problem, getting away from them is the answer. But, if I'm the problem, what is there to learn from this failed relationship? What's there for me to discover from this experience so that in the next relationship, I can make healthier choices?

You shock the rats at random for three weeks and at the end of three weeks, take them out of their cages and put them in water. What do you think Rat #1 does when you put him into water? He swims around looking for the safety of dry ground because he has learned, by virtue of his efforts, he can affect his destiny.

What about rat #2? What would you guess he would do when placed in the water? He doesn't try to swim to safety. He just treads water, trying to keep his nose above the surface to survive. We take him out before he goes down. Why doesn't he try to swim to high ground? Because he learned, it doesn't matter what he does, it doesn't make any difference. Why bother, it won't do any good . . . That's one depressed rat.

After the water experience the rats are examined. Rat # 1 is healthy but # 2, the depressed rat, has ulcers. Both rats get shocked with the same amount of electrical current, through their tails, for the same length of time. So, what is the difference?

Rat#1 has control. Is control occurring at the level of INput or response to INput? Response to INput. And being able to turn off the shock, did it keep the unfairness from happening again?

No. The shocking continued at random for the three weeks. That's a very sick environment. But, #1 stayed healthy even though the world he was placed in treated him very unfairly. He was stressed but he was also empowered. Rat #2, however, was in the unempowered role, the role of the victim. And in the role of the victim, he got sick.

If normal isn't healthy, that means many of the environments, at home, commuting, and at work, many of the environments that we function in may be normal but not particularly healthy. How can we be healthy in sick environments? That's the key. How can we be healthy when other people aren't?

We have to do what we can to stay out of the role of the victim. We have to empower ourselves even when others don't. We have to focus attention and energy where we have power and control. We then can break out of our old predictable patterns and begin to creatively live our lives, even when others don't. It may not be normal, but it is healthy.

CHAPTER 4

THE CAVE DWELLER LIVES (And Can Kill Us)

If we honor our feelings, they may be telling us something. But when we're so externally focused, obsessing about what the world has done to us, we can miss the message. The feelings are there, but because THEY made us feel like we do, we use our energy to try to get them to quit doing it to us.

If I say, "Gee, why am I feeling this way?" I can make a move toward a more positive way of responding. I can say, "I don't want to allow this difficult person to control my behavior or my mood. He is trying to manipulate me. What would be in my best interest? What would be a healthy choice?" In that psychological space, I can make a better response selection.

And why is it of value to do this? Well, the negative responses that we generate to stressful life events are not simply psychological. The body is a slave to the brain. What we do between our ears reflects itself as physiological change in the body. Our responses are psychophysiological events.

The stress response is a survival response. When you go through the stress response your body goes into a survival mode and a lot of things happen, driven by an adrenalin surge. We have the same bodies that our ancestors had when we were hunters and gatherers. When we get stressed, certain changes, physiological changes, go on inside that could end up making us sick.

Why? We're geared up for physical action, yet being physical may be inappropriate. It's like driving your car with one foot on the gas and one foot on the brake. If you drove your car like that, it wouldn't be long before you would be visiting your car doctor. The same is true of our physical body. If we drive it like that, it won't be long before we will be visiting the medical doctor with a stress related illness.

We talk about the pace of change. We talk about technology, how everything's moving faster. Well, let's go backward and think about what it was like when we were hunters and gatherers. The pace of life was much slower and simpler.

Let's say the females go picking berries. All of a sudden there is a great big she bear that appears from the other side of the bush as two young cubs scamper out. This would be a stressful event in the life of our ancestor and right in that moment, inside her body, the stress response kicks into high gear. She dumps high levels of adrenaline into her blood stream. She may be dumping other things other places. I'm sure I would. She instantly knows she is in deep trouble.

So what does she do? What's the stress response also called? Fight or flight response. Through the release of adrenaline, she's got the energy now to start running away or fighting the bear. She starts running away but the bear catches her. She rolls up into a ball trying to protect herself as the bear scratches, claws, and chews. Then the bear cubs run off. Mama bear releases our ancestor and follows her cubs.

So, here's our ancestor, our great, great, great, great, great, great grandmother, dazed on the ground. What just happened to her body in a very rapid period of time? This whole drama took only twenty seconds. The increase in adrenaline happens instantaneously. Immediately, blood goes out of the skin of the extremities into the muscles. Increased muscle tension results and then the muscles can do the extra work required to survive the threat, to fight or flee to safety.

Your muscles need oxygen to do their work and it is delivered by the blood. So the blood goes out of the skin into the muscles to give you extra muscle power to fight or flee, to survive. A side effect of that is that the blood is in the muscles and not in the skin when she gets scratched, clawed, and chewed. Hence, there is less blood loss.

There's something else that's happening simultaneously, which also is very useful. You have little cells in the body called platelets. And your platelets clump together when you get stressed. That's why some people suggest that you take an aspirin a day, because aspirin has this anti-platelet clumping affect. So her platelets are clumping together to help her keep from leaking all over the place and from bleeding to death.

What do you think happened to her blood sugar? It went way up. Why? She needd the energy. So the blood sugar has gone up and her platelets are clumping together. Her respiration's gone up. What other changes go on inside? Blood pressure goes up. Appetite goes down. Heart beats faster. What do you think happens to her immune defense system?

Well, it's interesting. The initial response of the immune defense system is to be activated. Why? Are those claws and teeth sterile? No. Bacteria are getting into the body, so the white blood cell mechanism is activated. Initially, then, the immune system is activated to deal with the acute invasion.

If you look at long-term stress, what happens? The immune defense system is depressed. They did a study, which looked at white blood cell function over time. The subjects were people who had been married a long time. When a spouse died, the researchers looked at white blood cell function in the surviving spouse, over the long term, including the time preceding the death.

Over time, the white blood cell function varied. When the spouse dies, you notice an initial enhanced immune response, increased white blood cell function followed by depressed white blood cell function. You have the same number of white blood cells, but they don't work as well. Under long-term stress, the adrenal glands produce corticosteroid hormones, which suppress immune function.

What do you think is happening to the surviving spouse? How have you heard people talk after they lose their mate of many years?

They're depressed. Have you ever listened to their use of language? "You know, I just don't know if I can go on without. . . ." And you know what? Their immune defense system is listening. There's a whole field now in medicine called psychoneuroimmunology. This field of study has to do with how our psychological state and our nervous system interacts with our immune defense system.

We know that white blood cells have, on their surface, receptor sites for neurotransmitters. When you think thoughts--remember those negative responses--you release little packets of chemicals called neurotransmitters: neuropeptides, neurohormones.

The illustration is a schematic of a white blood cell with an enlarged receptor site on the white cell surface.[graphic] What we know is that white blood cells have receptor sites for every single neurotransmitter we produce. We think thoughts, we release little packets of chemicals. We have receptors on our white blood cells for those neurotransmitters. Now, why should we have receptor sites for neurotransmitters on white blood cells, the disease fighting cells of the immune defense system?

It's the mind-body connection. This is one example of how psyche affects soma. The number of white blood cells is one thing of importance. But, their function, whether or not they work well, has a lot to do with our psychological state. Somebody wrote a book saying we can't afford the luxury of a negative thought. Me thinks that a little extreme and unrealistic. "Oh shit, I just had one! Now I wonder what sort of disaster will befall me. Oh, I have to change that one. Oh shit, too late."

So we have this mind/body connection which affects everything including the immune defense system. Think about cancer—all of us get cells that begin dividing abnormally and we have these white blood cells that ferret out abnormally dividing cells and get rid of them. Some of those tiny white blood cells are called lymphocytes.

I have shown patients a video of a cancer cell being attacked by white blood cells. What you see is a cancer cell with these little lymphocytes lined up along a section of its perimeter, eating a hole through the cell membrane. Inside is the nucleus of the cell. What the lymphocytes do once inside the cell is eat through the nucleus and destroy the cancer cell. Remember the term pseudopods? Amoeba have pseudopods, false feet, which can change their shape to allow the amoeba flow through their environment.

You've got these big white blood cells called macrophages, which also have false feet. That allows them to flow around the remains of the cancer cell and engulf the cellular debris. The end result--there is nothing left of the abnormally dividing cell.

Maybe we're all getting cancer all the time but our white cells are keeping those abnormally dividing cell from dividing and becoming a tumor. But when the white blood cells are not working right, we might grow a tumor instead.

Another big problem is heart disease, the number one killer here in the Excited States of America. Remember, when you go through the stress response your platelets clump together and your blood sugar increases. Blood sugar goes up to provide extra energy. Blood sugar provides a sticky adhesive for the clumping platelets. You always have blood fat, or cholestrol, in your blood stream. You make cholesterol in your liver. Even though you have a low cholesterol, you've always got cholesterol in your blood stream. If you've got the stickiness of blood sugar layered on the platelet clumps, fat can aggregate around this sticky substrate. And if you have a defect in one of your blood vessels, you can lay cholesterol plaque right into it and help clog your arteries.

We can explain 50 percent of heart disease on the basis of the risk factors for heart disease. Stress may have a lot to do with the other 50 percent. So these negative responses that we generate are normal but not healthy, not simply in the psychological sense but in a physiological one also. Mind and body are working together for good or ill all the time. So, going in a more positive response direction, is healthful in a lot of different ways.

Coming back to the closed loop system, where do we have power and control? When we move out of the role of the victim, we have power and control over how we choose to respond to life's INput. In other words, we only have control over OUTput. So if we focus energy and attention on this part of the system, we focus where we have power and control. We mentioned loss of control. Anytime time you feel as if you have no control over what's going on, it's exceedingly stressful.

Control—let me give you another example about control and stress. In the '60s, what was NASA's focus? The focus was putting somebody on the moon. There were people doing other projects at NASA, and guess what was happening to their funding? It was being cut.

There was an interesting, and unfortunate phenomenon that happened. Bright young engineers in their thirties were dropping dead of heart disease. A cardiologist named Robert Elliot was asked to go to Florida and help them deal with the problem. They couldn't figure out what was wrong with these people. When Elliot examined the hearts of the deceased, he found broken muscle fibers.

Those broken muscle fibers are called contraction band lesions. A lesion is a defect, and a contraction band is simply a muscle fiber. He found broken muscle fibers in the hearts of these people that had died. And he thought gee, that's weird. Because it's the same problem that you see in the hearts of people that die of pheochromocytoma. This is a tumor of the adrenal glands in which a person puts out high levels of adrenaline all the time.

So Elliot thought that high levels of adrenaline must have been present, but these people didn't have tumors of the adrenal glands. So he wondered what was the association. He wondered if just adrenaline itself, without a tumor, could be a problem. He put dogs in dog labs, injected adrenaline and noradrenalin into the dogs and sacrificed the dogs soon thereafter.

He found these broken muscle fibers in the hearts of the dogs. Then he went backward to try to find out what was going on with these engineers. That's when he found out the problems that they were working on were not connected to the landing on the moon. Because of budget cutbacks, their reward for doing their job well was to potentially those their job.

This was a situation over which they had no control. When the project was over, so was their funding. And if you're an engineer at NASA in the sixties, anyplace else you go is going to be a huge step down in terms of status, and recognition. By the way, lest you feel you've done irreparable damage to your hearts, these lesions repair themselves. They repair themselves if you give your body a chance to re balance. If you spend some time being quiet and balance the frenetic activity of our daily lives with some quiet time, the body repairs itself.

Let me give you another example of this control piece because it's fascinating. Earlier, we mentioned technology as a stressor. Test pilots have to be very healthy in order to fly experimental aircraft. They're called experimental aircraft for a reason. Why? The technology is not fully tested and may not work right. You have to be exquisitely healthy and pass rigorous physicals to be able to fly these aircraft.

There's a special little button on the throttle—a button for what? This is the panic button, the eject button to catapult the pilot's capsule free of a malfunctioning aircraft. The pilots are sometimes wired by telemetry to monitor their physiological function while flying the aircraft. If you're flying an aircraft, and you have a malfunction and you need to eject, you push the button.

What happens if the button doesn't work? You're not only dumping out high levels of adrenaline into the bloodstream, but you're also filling your shorts. Anyway, you push it, it doesn't work. You push it and you push it and it doesn't work. You then have the certain knowledge that you're going to die. What the scientists notice was that the pilots hearts stop beating before they hit the ground, before impact. They were literally scared to death. Findings at autopsy revealed contraction band lesions. How's that happen?

When you think about heart attacks—we were talking about platelet clumping and cholesterol and blood sugar combining to layer cholesterol plaque inside our blood vessels. That sequence of events can terminate in a heart attack. That is when a section of heart muscle dies because the blood vessel that provides nutrients and oxygen becomes blocked. The heart muscle beyond the blockage then necroses, or dies. If a large enough section of muscle dies, so does the patient.

There is another kind of heart death called a sudden cardiac death event. The heart transmits an electrical impulse through its musculature. If that impulse hits an area of broken muscle fibers, the beat may become aberrant—abnormal. Initially, the heart begins beating rapidly. Then the rhythm of the large chambers of the heart, the ventricles, may degenerate into something called ventricular fibrillation. Here, the heart is essentially is just quivering. It's not putting blood out into the great vessels. And that ventricular fibrillation will terminate in a sudden cardiac death event within a very brief period of time—three or four minutes at the max. But it can happen even quicker.

At autopsy, the hearts of people who die of sudden cardiac death events have contraction band lesions. So, what Elliot discovered was these young engineers were dying essentially from sudden cardiac death events. The same kind of heart events that test pilots have died from. And their stress wasn't a life-threatening situation—it was the loss of their job.

So the negative responses that we generate to stressful life events can make us sick. In fact, they can kill us. It may be normal to respond negatively when we get stressed. But, it obviously is not healthy.

CHAPTER 5

NUTWORKING

When we decide that we are going to begin responding in healthier ways to what life or other people put into our INbox, we can pay attention. Without the familiar stressful stimuli changing, the old patterns can be broken only if we pay attention. The flashlight of our attention moves from INbox to OUTbox. Energy follows attention. Paying attention to our responses, we have the energy required to generate change. Creative action then becomes an option in contradistinction to the old knee jerk reactions. Reaction implies no control. Action implies control.

Many of our responses to stressful stimuli are knee jerk in nature. When someone goes to the doctor and gets his reflexes checked, the doc bangs on the patellar tendon at the knee with a rubber hammer. That initiates a reflex arc, which travels from the knee, to the spinal cord and back to the knee again. The brain isn't in the loop. So if the doctor says, "I want you to think as hard as you can about this. When I bang on your knee, I don't want your knee to bounce up." It wouldn't help. Thinking doesn't stop the reflexive jerking of the knee because the brain isn't in the reflex arc. The patient has no control.

My feeling is that many of the responses we make to stressful situations reflect activity that is occurring somewhere below the level of the brain. The brain isn't in the loop. Therefore, control is exercised through the metaphorical hammers swung by others. But, once we become aware of that, we put the brain in the loop and can take back control. We can take action and through positive action, use our life stressors as fuel for growth and development.

35

Exercising that control over our response mechanism, means that people can no longer manipulate us so easily. When we are creatively responding to INput, thosewho have manipulated us in the past, may not be appreciative. Fact is, when we begin responding in healthier ways to what people place in our INbox, some people may wonder what's wrong with us.

How ironic, we do what is healthy and people wonder what's wrong. If your kids cannot get you to open up your wallet and dole out the green stuff because you want them to learn the value of the dollar, they're not going to like it. And explaining that you are just trying to be a healthier responder, may elicit, "bring back the sick guy. I liked him better."

Whenever we begin to operate differently in the field of action, we disturb the waters. It's the ripple effect. Creative action makes waves, ripples that go out to others that rock their world. Many people don't appreciate the new patterns of behavior because of the ramifications for them. When women first began to empower themselves to break out of the old cultural stereotypes and expand their role on the world stage, they rocked the boat. In family systems across the country there were rough seas. Men had to fix their own dinners or be hungry. Children learned how to do laundry or wore dirty clothes. It was a sea change that continues to wash around the world.

But that change was a force for the advancement of culture. Some would say it represented the first blow in the destruction of the family system. Not so. The reverse is true. The status quo was broken. But, it needed to be broken. The old way was for an old time, an anachronism, whose time had passed. Women releasing themselves from their cultural cages, represented the new idea whose time had come. Resistance was strong. But, the new idea was stronger. It marked a variation from the norm that was a better adaptation to the present world. That is how things evolve.

The implications of that variation have spread across the world. Thank God. But, resistance remains strong. "Power yields nothing without a struggle," said Fredrick Douglas, the former slave and Black senator in the post Civil War period.

What women did to accomplish this heroic task, they did together. They may have been alone in their family system as the only advocate for change. But, they banded together in consciousness raising support of each other outside of the purview of their nuclear families. Why? Because, normal isn't healthy. Even people who love us may not know how to give us healthy support. Women went outside of the family and met together to give and to get the healthy support they needed to do this difficult work.

For me, for anyone, to have the courage to break out of the old patterns and create something new, support is required. For me, for anyone, to have the courage to change and sustain the effort required to establish a new variation, healthy support is needed. Why? In the first place, it is hard to do the new and unfamiliar. It is easier to continue the familiar patterns even if they no longer work and are unhealthy.

Secondly, when doing something that we haven't done before, not only is it awkward, we may fall on our face. We may fail. And lastly, people in our own family system, friends, and coworkers may withdraw support when we no longer do what is predictable and familiar to them.

To have the courage to change, we need encouragement. Doing something that is difficult, we need healthy support to encourage us to get back up when we fail and try again. We can't expect just anyone, even our own family members, to fit the bill. They may know how to support us, but that support may have an "if clause" that isn't healthy. The conditions they place on their willingness to be supportive may be too restrictive. They may be doing the best job they can with the information they received from the culture about relationships and how to do support. They are doing what they learned to do from the grownups. But, how well did the grownups do relationships? How well did they do support?

Even in our primary love relationships, 50 percent of marriages end in divorce. Which is not to say that those people that stay married are necessarily in healthy, coequal, non-controlling, loving, affectionate relationships. Some people just stick it out.

"How long you been married?"

"How long have I been married? I dunno...seems like yesterday. Of course, you know what a miserable day yesterday was! Let's see, thirty years. Thirty years! Maybe Milton Berle was right. First there's the engagement ring, then the wedding ring, then the suffering." It may be normal, but it isn't healthy. It may be normal support, but it isn't healthy support.

So when I'm in the role of the victim, obsessing about some unfair INput, I don't want to stay in that role. It's an unempowered role and it's not healthy. It is going to make me sick. I want healthy support. If I'm going to respond in new ways to the familiar of my life, I want healthy support. But, I have to be selective where I look. Why? Because people can only do what they know.

They could be married to me. They could be a brother or sister. They could be my parent. They could be my friend and not know how to give me healthy support. You have to be selective. When I look for healthy support, I'm very selective where I look. I don't expect just anybody to be able to give it to me. Why? Because normal isn't healthy, the relational intelligence that most folks carry disqualifies them.

PREMATURE COGNITIVE COMMITMENTS

Do you know who the first Italian woman physician was? You have all heard her name.

Maria Montessori.

When we think about Montessori what do we think about?

School. She was an educator. Remember, physician is derived from a word that means medicine. Doctor is derived from a word that means teacher. Maria Montessori was an educator not a medicator. She was a giant, of immense importance, who has not fully received her due.

She wrote a wonderful book called the *Absorbent Mind*. We're born with absorbent minds, and we are absorbing from the get go—we are learning. That learning, initially, is unconscious. The organ of learning is the brain. When you look at how the brain works, it's very interesting. Most of the activity of the brain is spent inhibiting information flow.

Why would we want the organ of learning to spend most of its energy inhibiting information flow? It's bombarded with so much we would overload our circuits. So, the brain does two things. It filters some stuff out so we can focus the flashlight of our attention on one thing. It allows us to focus simultaneously as we filter. We filter some stuff out so we can attend to and focus on other stuff. We begin doing this from the beginning of the movie of our lives.

Let me ask you to free associate with this word, premature:

Babies, Death, Balding, Too early................

What I was thinking of and I'm sure it was going to be the next thing coming up for you, is premature cognitive commitments. Long before we're fully mature, when we're still babies, we begin to commit to certain ways of thinking about things. Cognition is simply about thinking. Long before we're fully mature we make premature cognitive commitments. We commit to certain ways of seeing self and world.

We're functioning in a relational field with other people, we're learning, and we're absorbing culture. We have an absorbent mind. We absorb culture and pass it on like a baton from generation to generation. The grownups pass it to us, we pass it to the next generation. We got some good stuff but we also got some stuff we probably don't want to pass along. I know there are certain things that I don't want to pass along.

But coming back to this process of learning, this process of focusing and filtering, when someone commits to a certain way of viewing self and world, things that do not fit with their set of biases are filtered out. That creates limits on their ability to perceive certain things. Those limits are called conceptual boundaries. We see certain things, believe certain things, and filter other things out. And if we don't believe something is possible, it isn't possible.

If we have made a premature cognitive commitment that being around a certain negative person means that we will feel bad, guess what? That's correct. It's a self fulfilling OUTput. We have to live with that limit. And we're living in the prison house of our conditioning.

Do you know the wonderful poet Rilke? Rilke was Rodin's secretary and wrote a poem called "The Panther." Do you know the poem? It's a great poem. Have you ever gone to the zoo and watched the great cats? What do the cats do? They just pace back and forth. And you go up and pound on the glass to get their attention. What do they do? They just keep pacing.

"From seeing and seeing the seeing no longer sees anything anymore. The world is made of bars a hundred thousand bars and behind the bars nothing. The lithe swinging of that easy rhythmical stride that slowly circles down to a single point is like a dance of energy around a hub in which a great will stands stunned and numb. At times a shape enters, slips past the tightened silence of the shoulders, enters the heart and dies."

That cat, when first placed in the cage, probably stopped and pounced when someone pounded on the glass. Initially, the cat hit the glass. But, over time the cat learned that it was of no use and now it just paces. "At times a shape enters, slips past the tightened silence of the shoulders, enters the heart and dies." Why bother to pounce? Why bother to take action? And the cat just keeps pacing.

The thing is, we're not like the panther. The panther has to wait for someone to open the cage. We can be free without anyone else unlocking the door. We have the key to let ourselves out. But there are going to be things that work against us. One of them is that it's going to feel awkward to do what's unfamiliar. Guess what a lot of prisoners do when they gain their freedom?

They go right back in.

Ever see *Shawshank Redemption*? A prisoner named Brooks was to gain his freedom but did not feel good about his future new circumstance. He didn't think that he could make it on the outside. He was an "institutional man." He had no support to prepare for his new life. So, he feigned a rule violation while still incarcerated so he could stay in prison. When he did get released he couldn't handle his freedom. As a free man, he took his own life.

We need support. We need healthy support. We're going to have to learn new behaviors because the old ones may have been normal but not healthy. What are the premature cognitive commitments we have made and the limits we have placed upon ourselves? What are we capable of doing? What are we not capable of doing?

When I was a freshman in high school I made a premature cognitive commitment that I was stupid. I think it had to do with flunking Latin, algebra, and typing. I also received a D- in Unified Studies, which was a combination of Social Studies, History, and English. My high water mark was a C in gym. I made a premature cognitive commitment, I was stupid. Guess what? My grades proved it. But I was functioning within a limit. And that limit was very powerful. And when you think you're stupid, guess what? You do stupid things.

(Subsequently, I learned that I'm not stupid. I'm slow but trainable. There isn't anything I can't learn. It may just take me longer than most. I also learned that that is also true for just about everybody else.)

Early on in our development, we are absorbing cultural biases. We are learning how to see self and world and we are pretty darned sure we're right. We call our set of biases "common sense." Ever notice that common sense is different for different people? "Well, she's a bright gal but she just doesn't have any common sense." Einstein said that common sense is the collection of prejudices that we have gathered by age eighteen. Remember when you were eighteen and pretty much knew it all?

The sponge-like quality of the young mind is indiscriminant. We had no control over what we absorbed. We can do the best job possible with the information we received. And we may be able to replicate culture but be unable to push it in a healthy direction. We'll just be able to replicate what we've gathered unless we face the limits of our own conditioning.

It's fascinating to look at this material phylogenetically. When we view natural evolutionary relationships, biological groupings go from very simple life forms to more and more complex organisms. And if you look at phylogenetic development, fleas and flies would be fairly low on the totem pole. Put fleas or flies in a jar and poke tiny little holes in the lid of the jar. Have them live in the jar for a while, then remove the lid of the jar. What do they do?

Most of them stay in the jar. There are just a few nuts that go over the edge. Most of them stay in the jar because the jar is their world. You remove the limit, and they stay with what they know. Just a few nuts go over the brim. If fleas could talk, imagine what those that stay in the jar would say about those that go over the edge. "Boy he's really gone over the edge." See, in our movement toward health, wholeness, emotional maturity, and freedom, you can't expect support from those that stay in the metaphorical jar.

In fact, your own growth can be threatening to those who stay put developmentally. And what they may want is to pull you back in. Because they're losing something that they know and what you're going off into they don't understand. So it's scary for them and they wonder, what's wrong with you? Come back in here with me. So what we have to do is find other nuts.

Right. It's a nutworking thing. Don't expect support from those who stay in the metaphorical jar. We must find other nuts to support us. One nut is a lot. Two is better, three is better, four is better. And when you start looking for nuts, guess what? You find them. You find nuts and you find the support that you need, but you have to be selective. You can't expect someone who stays in the metaphorical jar to know how to give you healthy support. In fact they may say, "What's wrong with you?" And withdraw support.

SOMETHING FISHY

Another example that demonstrates the power of our conditioning and the limits of past learning, can be seen with fish. Put fish in an aquarium and separate the aquarium with a transparent partition. Then, let the fish equilibrate to their respective sides of the aquarium. Then remove the partition. What do you think the fish do? Stay on their side. Why? That side is their world. That's what they know. They're doing what they learned. They've been to school. What happened when the barrier was in there? They got hurt. They smashed their little fish heads against the transparent partition and learned not to go over there. So they stayed safe doing what they learned.

How strong are these limits? Let's take pike and place them on one side of the aquarium, and minnows--pike food--on the other side. Let the fish equilibrate to their respective sides of the aquarium. The pike see the minnows. What do they do? They smash their heads against the glass trying to get at them. So they learn it's a trick. Now, remove the partition. Are the little fishes going to swim over to visit the pike? No way Jose. So, they on their side. The pike, likewise, stay on their side . . . and starve, doing what they learned. They starve in the face of abundance. Doing what they learned, they don't know how to act in their own best interest.

I think that's also true of humans. We can do the best job with our life with the information we got and not know how to act in our own best self interest. People can be in an abusive relationship, but, it's familiar. They know it. They play out worst-case scenarios that will happen if they take the risk of doing what's unfamiliar and leave. They're breathing, still have their chest pain, but they are breathing. Whatever their symptoms are; palpitations, back pain, head aches, lets them know they're alive. They are surviving.

But, there's this possibility that with healthy support they can swim into the new. Most of stress management is about staying on your side of the metaphorical aquarium with an increased level of comfort. It's about moving from negative stress responses to more positive coping behaviors, so that you now cope with stress with healthy behaviors. And you know what? If your marriage isn't working, go work out. If your relationship isn't working, meditate. By coping, we can avoid dealing with what we need to deal with. We can avoid changing by coping. Coping with the status quo is the antithesis of change.

What we really want to do, what I'm really interested in doing, is not simply coping with the status quo in healthy ways. I want to use the stressors of my life as a stimulus to change. I'm interested in swimming to the other side of the metaphorical aquarium. I'm interested in swimming into the new and knowing that if I'm going to do that, I've got healthy support. Which means I'm going to hang out with someone that's been swimming over there who can mentor me. Or, I want some other nut to take the plunge with me.

And we know that change is possible. A good therapist, working with an individual, can help that individual take the journey into the new. But you don't always need a good therapist. What you may need to do is know how to act in your own best self interest and find other nuts that are going to give you healthy support. Other nuts are going to encourage you to do what's required to be healthy. For me to have the courage to change I really need encouragement. Because it's easy to fall back into old familiar patterns of response conditioned into me by culture.

The prison house may have bars on the doors but they're familiar, it's home. People are fed three squares daily. It's survivable. And we just keep pacing . . . . We need other nuts to remind us when they see us just going through the paces.

It's important to be selective where we look for support. Some people think the way to support you is to help you stay stuck where you are with a friend. "Oh, man, that is bad. I don't blame you for being upset. I'd be upset too if that happened to me. And because I want to support you, not only am I going to bum myself out too. I'm going to help you sustain a low. Come on, maybe we can ruin the entire day." Gee, thanks . . . rather, no thanks.

Likewise, if someone is trying to tell you what and how to do everything, you want to question whether that's healthy support. I think what you really want—what I want—is someone to hold up a mirror and reflect back what they see. And if I'm in a stuck place, let me know that honestly. But I don't just want the honesty. Honesty alone has a very sharp edge. "You want honest? I'll give you honest." I want honesty to be coupled with compassion. I want some warmth coming out of their body to me. I want to feel some warmth. If I don't feel any warmth, I'm likely to filter out what they say.

One of the things I do is ask people how many good teachers they've had in their lives. In a group I ask them to hold up the number of fingers of really good teachers they've had. I'm talking about actual teachers in school that are paid professionals. This is their job. Part of normal not being healthy is I rarely see anybody using two hands. What was it about these teachers that made them really good?

They cared. They had some passion for their profession and they really cared about their students. Did it mean they were always easy on us? No. Did it mean they always said what we wanted to hear? No! But one felt their warmth. We felt they cared. They also, at times, believed we were capable of things we didn't feel capable of. Goethe had a wonderful statement about the treatment of others. He said that if we treat other people the way they are, they stay that way. If we treat other people the way they are capable of becoming and they become that which they are capable of.

When we are looking for healthy support, nutworking should provide us with honesty coupled with caring, and a belief that we can change even when we fail and fall on our face. I have been interested in the material presented here for many years. I have been a recovering normal person , actively pursuing a healthier life and relationships with self and others, for a long time. And I have made some progress. But, I have psychological narcolepsy.

I can fall psychologically asleep in a nanosecond and forget everything I know. I can revert back into the old predictable knee jerk response pathways and play the role of the victim in short order. So, I need healthy support. With that

47

kind of support, I can do what is difficult. I can accept responsibility without blaming others for my lot in life. And when I forget what I know and revert back into the old reactive modis operandi, I know what I have to do. Be needy.

As a doctor, people honor me when they allow me to treat them. They allow me to participate in their lives in a meaningful way. Guess what I do when I allow someone else to support me? I honor them. I allow them to participate in my life in a meaningful way. And guess what? They like it. So, I have given myself permission to be needy.

As a member of the medical profession, I am supposed to be the one who tends the needy. As a medical doctor, when people come to me they allow me to use my gifts in the service of others. This, likewise, is true when I allow someone else to "doctor" me. I allow them to use their gifts in the service of another human being. Whether I'm psychologically awake or asleep, my healthy friendship circle of support will be there to serve whenever I need them. They will give me healing words of encouragement to be the change I want to see in the world and hand me a pair of flippers for the swim into the new.

CHAPTER 6

USING STRESS TO POWER PEAK PERFORMANCE

Referring back to Goethe above, what are we capable of? We know we're capable of screwing up. We know we're capable of not meeting our own expectations or those of others. We know we are capable of reacting negatively to life. But what are we capable of in a positive sense? I made a premature cognitive commitment when I was kid that I was stupid. And then I did stupid things. My report cards proved what I knew. It was hard science.

Obviously, I went to medical school so something happened. What happened was that I discovered something. I discovered that I was slow but trainable, not stupid. I could learn anything it just took me longer than some other people. I also found that a lot of the "truths" that people tell you are not true when tested. We've probably all heard things that we believed and never tested that now are part of our belief system. We need to question and examine those beliefs and consciously decide what to keep and what to discard.

I think an ounce of prevention is worth a pound of cure. I don't want to wait for a big enough stressor in my life that breaks the status quo and leaves me with no choice but to do something new. I want to use the smaller, familiar stressors in my life as a stimulus for change. That way the status quo will always be changing, for life will always be stressful.

Some of you are familiar with Paul Azinger. He's a pro golfer. What happened to Paul Azinger?

He got cancer. He was very successful, very good at what he did. When we were kids growing up, what did we hear that we had to do to be really good at what we did . . . hard work.

Hard work was the key. The secret to success, when we were growing up was hard work.

Did the grownups say to the children studying their lessons or doing their chores, "You know, you kids aren't playing enough. If you really want to get ahead in this world, I think you should be playing more." Hardly.

Of course, in competitive sports, play is turned into work. Azinger worked hard, was a good golfer and won one of the major professional championships, the PGA tournament. He'd been working hard and was very successful. Then, he got cancer. A year after he got cancer he was interviewed on television. I saw the interview. Guess what he said about getting cancer?

It was the best thing that ever happened to him.

The best thing that ever happened! Do you think that was his first response? Do you think the doctor came in and said, "Well, Mr. Azinger, it is cancer." "Cancer, what kind? Lymphoma. Oh, boy! I was hoping for that!" But a year later, it was the best thing.

It was a significant, world-stopping event.

He'd been working hard hitting a white thing around a green place, into a hole. And he was really good at what he did. All of a sudden he gets cancer and the status quo is broken. He can't keep doing what he did before. So the flashlight of his attention shifts. Immediately he saw the familiar with new eyes and saw what was most important in his life. Maybe there was a connection with his children that he hadn't fully honored, likewise with his spouse. He made a

50

deeper connection with others and with his highest, most deeply held values. He did something new in response to having the status quo broken.

Some might say he had no choice. But that is not so. He could have played the role of the victim, played poor me and stayed stuck in the slough of despair. I don't want to wait for the significant world-stopping life event. I'd like to use the little stressors when they come up, the smaller ones, as effectively as possible, to get me to swim into the new. I want to cope in healthy ways. But coping isn't enough.

I can stay stuck in my life, doing what I already know with an increased level of comfort, by using healthy coping strategies. I want to use my stressful life events, the unfairnesses when they occur, to stimulate my development and the unfolding of my giftedness. I think, because normal is not healthy, it's hard to do that unless we have had significant trauma.

If we have overt dysfunction, there's something there to support us—treatment centers, support groups, hospitals. But without overt dysfunction, there isn't really a network, a nutwork, out there at the moment. So we have to create our own.

Because a lot of what we're talking about isn't part of our dialogue, isn't part of our awareness, we can't utilize certain things that would be helpful by way of having a safety net. And it's connected back to the support piece. The nutwork is the safety net. It encourages our risk taking, healthy behaviors, so we feel safe enough to confront the reality of our stressful lives.

You see it so much in the papers or on TV. Some major trauma or event happens to someone or a family member. The recipients of the INput mobilize

51

energy and start a new cause or new passion, which is wonderful, but it's so unfortunate that it had to happen after someone died or got ill.

Bill W., cofounder of Alcoholics Anonymous, called it the awful grace of God.

It opens up their life, and good things can come of it and do frequently. But it usually happens after the fact.

They have been pushed by their life circumstances to let go and jump full force into reality and the net appears…or wings.

The way of love is not a subtle argument

The door there is devastation

Birds make great sky circles of their freedom

How do they learn it

They fall and in falling they are given wings

Rumi

Rumi, is my favorite poet at this time in my life. Rumi was an old poet born in 1207 in what's now Afghanistan and lived most of his life in Konya, Turkey at the end of the silk road. He was an amazing poet. He would spontaneously emit poems. And students would write down what he said and he'd do maybe ten poems a day. He spoke in Persian and there'd be several rhyming words in each line. The best translator of his poetry is Coleman Barks. If you like what you read here of Rumi's poetry, Barks' translations are exquisite. Read them. Fact is, although it wouldn't be normal, it would be healthy to get one of his books and read it daily. When finished, get another. That's a great way to stay in touch with what it means to be healthy.

Referring back to the example of Paul Azinger, there was a piece that I did not bring up that I think would be useful on this journey. It allows us to see, at the deepest levels, we are all connected at the center through our values. Then, we can see past our differences while honoring them, and note the value of the unfairness of life. Anybody know, by the way, what the definition of a sufi is?

Sufi's are the mystical Moslems . The mystical sufi tradition within Islam is very powerful. And mystics in any religious tradition talk the same way. They talk about having an experience of something now, versus getting a lollipop when they croak. One definition of sufi is: the person that finds the joy that comes from sudden disappointment. Now that's not easy. Buddhist's use the phrase, to joyfully participate in the suffering of the world. A friend and mentor of mine, Elmer Green, and I were talking about this once, and he said, "You know Bowen, the real trick is to joyfully participate in your own suffering." Thank you Elmer, zapped again.

The devastation that Paul Azinger experienced allowed him to find his wings and fly out of the metaphorical jar of his conditioning. Isn't it interesting how the significant event alarm awakens us to pay attention and expend energy in new ways.

Let's talk more about the unfairnesses of life and how they may serve us, tying it back into our rat science. This time we are going to take three genetically identical rats. Rat# 1 and Rat # 2 will be hooked up as in the previous experiment. Rat #1 is empowered and #2, unempowered. But now we're going to have a rat that has the same kind of wire, but receives no shock. In other words, this is a genetically identical rat to the other two. There's a wire around the tail. Everything else is the same, but this rat does not get shocked because the wire is not connected to the electrical device. He doesn't get the unfairness in the INbox that the other two get.

There is unfairness, however, in that we're going to give all three rats cancer. We're going to give all three rats cancer and monitor cancer growth to see which rat can best defend against cancer. So, we'll shock rats #1 and #2 at random and rat #3 won't get shocked at all. We're going to see how their immune defense systems handle the cancer that we give them. Now, had you not read the previous material on rat science, what would you guess would be the rat that could best defend against the cancer? What do you think most people would guess would be the rat that would have the <u>least</u> amount of cancer growth?

Rat # 3, the one not getting shocked at all because he's not getting stressed like the other two. What rat would have the <u>most</u> cancer growth?

Rat # 2, the unempowered rat. Which one would be in the middle? Rat # 1.

When you do the experiment you find out that Rat #2 does have the most cancer growth, but Rat #1 has the least. The one that doesn't get any shock at all, Rat # 3, is in the middle. Rat #3 has more cancer growth than the one who gets shocked but can turn off the shock. Rat #1 is the empowered rat.

Rat #1 must be mobilizing some potential within him that Rat #3 cannot access without being stressed. Anytime we feel as if we have no control over what's going on it is exceedingly stressful. So the more that we feel we have some measure of control, the more empowering it is, not only in a psychological sense but in a physiological one.

Rat #1's immune defense system works better than #3 who is not getting shocked at all. Why is there pain and suffering and unfairness in the world? And, of course, patients have said this to me, maybe you've had the same experience, "If there really is a God, how can this happen?" I don't know how to answer that. In general, I think it best to just speak for myself. M.D. doesn't stand for <u>M</u> <u>D</u>iety. But maybe it has to do with getting in touch with some potential within us that we would not otherwise discover.

The fact is, we can't reach peak performance without being stressed. A better question may be, what's the purpose or meaning? When we look for the meaning, we often find it and learn something useful for our own evolution. Looking for and finding meaning is a variation from the norm, which provides for a better adaptation to an unfair world.

A great example of the experience of unfairness and finding meaning is Victor Frankl who wrote, *Man's Search For Meaning*. It's a great classic, written after he was released from a Nazi concentration camp. He was a Jewish psychiatrist and had been in the camp for two years. He gets out of camp and writes the book in nine days. He doesn't want his name on the book because he doesn't care about recognition. It's a gift to all of us about what he learned during two years in Hell.

What he found out is the Germans had control: when he ate, when he slept, when he worked, how he worked, what he wore. They determined what went into his INbox. They had total control. Well, almost total. He said there was one thing that they couldn't control: his attitude about what was happening to him. And by focusing on that one thing that he could control, how he responded to INput, he found meaning. And he found meaning in the worst of circumstances.

Okay, if he can do that in a German concentration camp, come on, what about us. We live in fantasyland. When we think about what much of the planet is experiencing right now, it's not central heat and hot water. We have such abundance. One half of the planet doesn't even have easy access to potable water, let alone hot water out of the faucet. We get to enjoy the accoutrements of a very high standard of living. But what do we do? We play the role of the victim.

Where's the meaning? We have a goal-oriented society where everybody focuses on success. Frankl wrote a foreword to a late edition of the book and in it he said that it was ironic, he had written a bunch of books. But this book sold many millions of copies, many more than any other he had written. And he wasn't going to even put his name on it. He didn't want the flashlight of collective attention to be on him.

Rather he wanted people to focus on the content and place the flashlight of their attention on themselves and their own attitudes about life. His name ended up being placed on the title page, it wasn't on the outside of the book. He said, "Maybe success is like happiness. It happens precisely because you decide not to think about it."

Interesting idea. Maybe happiness is like success. It happens precisely because we decide not to think about it. If we focus on getting happy directly, we look for the "fix" that will accomplish the goal. We focus on INput. What do we have all over the country, from five to seven p.m.? Happy hour! Booze is the number one stress management tool in our culture. And, it is very popular on the global scene.

If you pursue happy directly, you end up moving in the direction of an addictive disorder. It's part of the deal. The problem is, it works. It does change the way we feel. It alters mood.

But the idea of living your life in a healthy way, a way that's fulfilling, means you're going to experience the fullness of life. That means, the fullness of joy and also the fullness of your pain. Feeling better, really means feeling your feelings better and not medicating away the pain. Experiencing the pain allows us to make a connection to other people that we wouldn't have otherwise made through our own life experience. And that connection is not something that we honor, because it might mean that we would then not be able to bury our heads in the sand, when we are exposed to the suffering of humanity.

Speaking of stress management, let's talk about a healthy coping skill. Let's say, for instance, you can no longer drink alcohol. You no longer can use, not just your drug of choice, you can no longer use any mood altering substance. So you lost your old stress management tool, and no longer use what you were using to cope. So it needs to be replaced with something else.

Well, how do you turn off the stress response and turn on the relaxation response? You can actually learn how to do that without any chemicals. Our bodies generate chemicals all the time; we are chemical factories. We can learn to produce relaxation chemicals without taking a pill. One tool we can use is biofeedback. And one of the things we do in stress recovery workshops is spend time self-quieting. We talk about psychophysiology and the mind/body connection.

People are given a little temperature device that they put on their finger and it gives them a digital readout of their skin temperature. When you're relaxing, your hands are warming. Why? Because you move blood out of your muscles, since it's not needed for fight or flight. You don't need extra strength, so blood comes out of the muscles into the skin and your hands warm when you relax. So they each get a little temperature biofeedback device and begin to learn how to warm their hands.

You can't try hard to warm you hands. If you go, "Man, I'm going to warm my hands. I'm really gonna warm them." You will stress yourself and your hands will probably cool. You have to let go of trying hard in order to be able to warm your hands.

You have an intention of what you would like to have happen, i.e. to have your hands warm. But you don't try to force it to happen. The part of your will that you're training is called your passive volition. Active volition, the active aspect of will, is this domineering part of us, "Well I'm going to go out there and make that happen, kick butt, take names." That's the active part of your will.

Passive volition, the passive aspect of will, works by creating an environment to allow something to happen and it happens. It happens, not by force of will, (not actively) but because you allow it to happen (but passively). And, of course, it all ties right back in with the whole idea of letting go and letting God. In other words, surrender.

I think that is an important piece. There's a freedom that comes from allowing things to happen at their own pace, and not by virtue of our force of will. We know addicts can't quit using their medicative behaviors by virtue of willpower. The whole idea is to get help.

Do we have to wait until we get help? No. Learning to relax as a life skill allows us to do something to help ourselves. Besides, some people don't have a belief system inclusive of a Higher Power. Well, guess what happens if you can get them to sit down and be quiet? Maybe that's what they need to do is just sit down and be quiet. Guess what happens when people actually spend time being quiet? They connect. "Silence is not the absence of sound, but the absence of self." (DeMello, pg.142, One Minute Wisdom.) We empty the self and contact what?

There's the possibility that some connection may happen. You can't control it. I had a friend Don Campbell who got up every morning and spent an hour being quiet. He'd spend some time reading and then he'd just be quiet. And he said what he was doing was going to God's waiting room. He would go in there and wait. Sometimes God would show up, sometimes not. But, by God, he was in the waiting room, just in case. When we quit using other things to fill the hole inside, God rushes in. It's really a God-shaped vacuum. We empty the self of the self. What's left?

Active volition is really that egocentric part of us that wants things to happen at our pace. It resonates with worldly power, dominating power. If we *empty* that part of us out, then we're *open* to allow something else to fill the vacuum:

Jars of spring water are not enough anymore

Take us down to the river!

The face of peace, the sun itself.

No more the slippery cloud like moon.

Give us one clear morning after another

59

And the one whose work remains unfinished,

Who is our work as we diminish, idle,

Though occupied, empty and open.

Rumi (Barks)

With our own pain and suffering, perhaps life is trying to get our attention. Maybe there's something that we're going to get out of the experience, like Rat #1. In physics, as in life in general, there is potential energy and kinetic energy. The difference between these two is that potential energy is energy at rest. Kinetic energy is energy in motion. I believe that we have some potential inside us at rest. When we get stressed, get healthy support and focus on doing the things that we can do to be healthy, we're putting something that may have been at rest, into motion.

Rat #1 had large stressors, initially the shock and then the big one, cancer. But I don't think we have to wait for a "big one" to take our potential and put it into motion, into action. If we can use everyday stressors and not play the role of victim, we can tap more of our potential.

How will you know the difficulties

Of being human, if you're always

Flying off into blue perfection?

Where will you plant your grief-seeds?

Workers need ground to scrape and hoe,

Not the sky of unspecified desire

Again, we have the right to complain, bitch, and moan because life is unfair. It's not that we're unsympathetic to people who are suffering. But there's a way of being with people who are suffering where we're not simply trying to help them sustain a low. Rather it's a matter of being with them in a way that allows them to make a connection, to connect to the meaning, for them, of their current life circumstance.

And sometimes people just need to make that connection and thereby have a new awareness to make healthier choices. Then they can put into action their own potential energy and plant their "grief seeds."

-- REEL ONE OF THE MOVIE--

CHAPTER 7

RUNNING THE UNIVERSE

I like to think about life as a movie. We start the movie externally referented, externally focused. And we learn to live in reference to what's occurring in our environment. Actually we learn to focus on what's going on with our producers because these are the people in our environment who have the flashlight of our attention. We focus. We see these giants out there. Actually we might focus on one part of one of the giants.

Piaget and Freud said to an infant the world is a thing to suck. The fact is, when you go to examine a newborn baby you do something called the APGAR exam. You check for pulse, respiration, skin color, muscle tone, and suck reflex. You stick your pinky in their face to see if the newborn sucks on your finger. If the suck reflex is not intact, the child has a significant neurological deficit. So to an infant the world is a thing to suck. We come in sucking the world.

Physical food then comes from the outside in. And look at the dynamic. We move from empty to full by virtue of consumption. So, the emptiness inside is filled from the outside in. We're unconsciously learning that when something is missing inside, the something that we are missing comes from outside, the environment. We need physical food to survive. In order to let the giants know it's time to fill up the tank with physical food what do we do? Cry. And when we cry we control the giants to feed us.

So we start out the movie of our life learning that we run the universe. Have you noticed, it's exhausting work running the universe? It's so tiring trying to keep all the planets in orbit. The problem is, that sometimes it works. We cry.

We get fed. We need physical food. What else do we need from the giants? We need emotional food.

Emotional food is like physical food. It comes from the outside in. What do we have to do to get emotional food? Cry. It works. It works early in the movie, but later crying doesn't work anymore. Family docs and Pediatricians teach parents to let their infants cry at night so the parents can get some rest. So, we have to find another way to get emotional food. What we learn to do is tune into the parents and give a pleasing performance for our producers. We learn how to perform, to give a pleasing performance for them and then, they give us warmth, emotional food.

So, we learn to be who other people need for us to be to meet their needs. Everything depends upon them. We're not adequate to get what we need without them. So, we tune into them and figure out what we have to do, to get what we need from them. (So, over time, we learn to be who other people need for us to be to meet their needs.) The flashlight of our attention is externally focused. We learn to be people-pleasers. We have an external reference for our internal process. We're externally referented and internally neglectful.

We didn't start out internally neglectful. We were very demanding. We stood up for ourselves. We shouted. We cried. We did whatever we had to, to get what we needed. But, over time, we learned in the process of our development, how to perform on the world stage. We learned how to be who other people needed us to be to meet their needs.

This is called compliance. Do you know another word for the compliant child? Well behaved. Good boy. Good girl. Oh, what a little lady you are. What a little gentlemen you are.

Another term for this would be incongruent. Another term for this would be proper. To have an acute sense of propriety means to tune into what's going on in your environment and then do what's proper.

When I was a little kid, I was a boy scout. "On my honor, I promise to do my best, to do my duty, to God and my country, and to obey the scout law. To help other people at all times, to keep myself physically fit, mentally awake, and morally straight. A scout is trustworthy, loyal, helpful, friendly, courteous, kind, obedient, cheerful, thrifty, brave, clean, and reverent."

A scout does his duty to God and to his country, and helps other people at all times. In the front of my boy scout manual was a boy scout saluting the American flag and behind him it said, "I'm third." Didn't some of us get that in our religious training? God's first, everybody else is second, and I'm third? We learn to be externally focused and internally neglectful.

The good boy scout becomes a true gentleman. I went away to college, joined a fraternity, and we had to memorize something called "the true gentleman." "The true gentleman is a man whose conduct proceeds from goodwill and an acute *sense of propriety*. Whose self control is equal to all emergencies. Who does not make the poor man conscious of his poverty, the obscure man of his obscurity, or any man of his inferiority or deformity. Who is himself humble when necessity compels him to humble another. Who *thinks of the rights and feelings of others rather than his own*. And who appears well in any company. A man with whom honor is sacred and virtue safe."

This is supported by culture. We get acculturated. We absorb it. And we learn to be externally referented and internally neglectful. The boy scout becomes the true gentleman. The scout learns "I'm Third." The true gentleman "thinks of the rights and feelings of others, rather than his own" and has "an acute sense of propriety". We do what's proper, but we're incongruent.

We repress how we think and feel, and we express only what's safe to say. Anybody else have that experience in their family? Anybody know what happens when you repress how you think and feel and express only what is safe to say? What's the implication if you repress yourself? Psychically, what am I doing? I'm putting myself down, depressing myself.

We're pushing ourselves down. Has anybody heard of the Incredible String Band from the 1960s, out of the Scottish Highlands? They made some wonderful music. There's a lyric from an old song that goes something like: Queen Cleopatra, Richard the Lion Heart, the Butcher, the Baker, the Candlestick Maker, we've all settled down in one ship together. Troubled voyage in calm weather.

The weather outside isn't the problem. It's weather in the home, inside, under the roof, inside us that is nettlesome.

We look for a "fix" for the internal, inclement weather. We're looking for some way to take care of this depression and putting ourselves down. We're looking for ways to feel better. There are a number of things out there that work temporarily. I'm talking about addictive, medicative behaviors. Rather than deal with what our current feelings are trying to teach us, we look for the "fix" that we've learned is outside, and bring it inside.

Rather than rock the boat, by saying what we think and feel and taking authentic risks, we stay safe. Rocking the boat would be counter to survival.

I have this wonderful friend who happens to be lawyer. He is an incredibly creative person. He plays great ragtime piano. He draws great cartoons. He's incredibly funny. But he's a lawyer, trying to support his family, so, he does foreclosures. Although he really is good at what he does, he wants to do something else. He is trying to get into mediation.

But he has this problem. He says, "I have two friends that will never desert me. Wherever I go, wherever I am, I wake up in the middle of the night, they are there for me: denial and avoidance. They are always there wherever I go. And if I no longer can deny something, I will avoid it." Avoidance goes nicely with denial. Add one to the other and they go together synergistically. I'm very familiar with these two, how about you?

But that's normal. Now is there any other term for this: externally focused, internally neglectful, inauthentic, incongruent, yet controlling type of person? Codependent.

The definition of codependency is to be externally referented. When externally referented, you're focusing on what's occurring around you and being driven by it. The actively drinking alcoholic, who is dependent on booze, comes into the house and drives the mood of the rest of the family. The rest of the family is externally referented, monitoring the dependent person, to determine their own behavior. Is it safe to get close, or should I stay away?

The codependent's mood is driven by the mood of the one dependent on alcohol. The behavior and mood of the active drinker, even when he's not drinking, drives the mood of the family because the family is still codependent. We were born dependent. Then we're taught to be codependent. We live our lives trying to be who other people need for us to be to meet their needs. And can die without ever knowing who we really are. It's an uplifting thought. NOT!

I was working with a forty-eight-year-old stockbroker who came to see me with high blood pressure. And we were talking about family systems including this idea of compliance and codependency. And he said, "You know what you're talking about doesn't have anything to do with me." And I said, "Tell me about it." He said, "Well, when I was a kid growing up, I didn't run around trying to please my parents. In fact, I couldn't please my parents."

I said, "Go on." He said, "Well, I was a little league baseball player. I was a pitcher and I was good. In one little league game I struck out nineteen of twenty-one batters." There's only twenty-one outs in a little league game. I said, "That's unbelievable. That's not just good, that's great!"

"That's not what my dad said. He said, "C'mon son, we need to work harder. You just don't quite get it do you?" You can imagine his dad probably didn't want him to get a big head. He didn't want his kid to quit working hard.

The broker went on, "I lived in Indiana and when I was a freshman in high school I made the all state freshman basketball team." (What's the religion in Indiana? Basketball.) "Wow, a great baseball and basketball player, that's outstanding." "That's not what my dad said." He said, "Freshman team son, that's not even varsity, c'mon son, you can do better."

I told him that I found that sad. He said, "It wasn't so sad. When I was in senior in high school, I didn't even go out for sports." I said, "you were a great athlete already, both in baseball and basketball. You probably could have received a scholarship. Why didn't you go out for sports?" Why do you think he didn't go out for sports? Whatever he did was never going to be good enough. That hurt. How could he get back at his dad, whom he couldn't please?

By *not* playing. Instead of being compliant, he becomes defiant. He was in rebellion to his father. So, he was defiant to authority but he had a peer group with whom he was now hanging that said, "Way to go. I wish I could have seen his face," because his dad totally freaked out. "Cool man!"

The irony is, rebellion and compliance are two sides of the same coin. The reference for behavior is still external. And, he is internally neglectful because he really wanted to play on the school team. He didn't honor his own needs, he didn't act in his own best self interest, because he was codependent with his father and with his peers. He didn't want to have to deal with his father's lack of support.

He didn't go out for sports because his father wanted him to. He and his father were in a dance and his father was leading. And while he's rebelling to authority, he's being compliant with a peer group. So compliance and rebellion are two sides of the same coin. The rebel is just as codependent as the compliant child, even though he is noncompliant to the authority figure.

These are our choices: good boy or bad boy; good girl or bad girl; compliant or defiant. The problem is, that's not enough choices. But having a peer group that accepts us and sees us as adequate is really wonderful physic compensation for feelings of inadequacy. Kids want to be accepted by a group. Then they experience the power of the group. Having group power, they feel safer, more okay.

The freshman girl gets asked out by the junior halfback of the football team. What happens to her status in the eyes of her peers when the cool guy asks her out? It goes up. "Wow! You are so lucky. He is so cute." They go out on a few dates and he starts hitting on her to perform sexually for him. If she doesn't comply, he will drop her. What then would happen to her status in the eyes of her peers? It would go down. So she wonders, "Do I do what he wants me to do to meet his needs?"

I think we ought to be talking about this. It is great psychic compensation for her feelings of inadequacy to be asked out by this cool guy. It makes her okay. If he drops her, then she's not. If her value and worth is determined by his attention, when she no longer is in his flashlight, she is devalued. If she valued herself enough she could better withstand social pressures. Even if she hadn't learned to value herself more, if she understood the dynamic at work, she could make a healthy choice.

The environment provides the "fix" to turn the interior minus into a plus for both our physical and emotional needs. And all our addictive behaviors are related here. They change how we feel. Chemical dependency is only one of them.

Relationships can be addictive. The middle-aged male wonders if he's still attractive to women. It works both ways. Gee, here she is, a fifty-year old woman. And someone starts hitting on her. Whoa! How's that feel? Feels pretty nice. "He's actually paying attention to me!" We're set up to have somebody else validate us. Why? Because we're normal. And we have our neediness that hasn't been addressed. We don't take the flashlight of our attention and shine it on us. It's not part of our awareness.

So in reel one of the movie, we learn to be who other people need for us to be to meet their needs. And if we can give a pleasing performance to others and have them affirm us, it's great psychic compensation for any feelings of inner lack. If they're giving us a plus, we don't feel like such a minus. It helps us feel better.

It also means in our relationships, we may only say what we think others want to hear. What I learned to do is to focus on what's going on with those people around me and to do what's proper. And for person A; I ought to be A. And for person B; I ought to be B. And for person C; I ought to be C. You know what I'm saying here don't you?

Have you seen the movie *Zelig*? The character that Woody Allen plays is a human chameleon. He changes his color to match the environment. If he's around Fidel Castro, all of sudden he looks like Castro. If we're learning to be who other people need for us to be to meet their needs that means we become an alphabet of us for an alphabet of others. I know how to do that, and guess what? It's exhausting.

It's exhausting to have to be an alphabet of me for an alphabet of you. It's much less stressful for me now to be one person for all people. I can do it when I'm awake and feeling okay with my not okayness. But when I doze of on autopilot, I forget and revert to being an alphabet soup of a person.

Shakespeare said it: "To thine ownself be true." But it's not easy to be true to yourself.

What's worse? Is it worse to give up part of who we are to be liked by other people or validated by them; or to be true to ourselves, truly ourselves, and risk the loss of esteem in their eyes?

Here's the paradox: When we try to be who other people need for us to be to meet their needs; when we allow them to determine our grade in life, our esteem in their eyes goes down. It doesn't go up. In the extreme, that's the "yes man."

That's the irony. When we are authentic, when we are real, because it's so uncommon, other people notice there's something about us that's different, engaging. They may see you as an iconoclast or eccentric. That doesn't necessarily have a negative charge. Think back to Gandhi. He's real, true to himself, and nonviolent. He leads India toward independence from Britain's colonial rule in traditional Indian clothing.

He is put in a position to go around and meet world leaders. Ever see him in a suit? I don't remember seeing him in a suit. Do you think these world leaders ever talked about him behind his back? Maybe they did, but I don't think he was worried about it. And we're still talking about him. And who aren't we talking about who was around then? The guys in the suits. That's the paradox. When our concern involves building esteem in the eyes of others, we don't get what we want through that effort. We trick ourselves. It's a con. But, we buy the con.

"When I took the risk of just being myself, people who I really liked came into my life. The people that really should have been in my life were there. And all these other people who I didn't connect with anyway, didn't come so close. So I didn't have to get rid of them. When you are yourself the right people are in your life. That's who you relate to. Like attracts like," So said Alex, a bright thirty-eight-year-old woman, in a recent discussion. People call that the law of attraction.

I think there's something to that. When I think about some of the things I've done, they are certainly related to my ego and the desire to be held in high regard. When my concern is for my image in the eyes of other people, what part of me is driving my behavior? My ego. And I can't pretend I don't have one of those. We all have one, that's part of the deal. But, how can we have a healthy ego? Well, we esteem ourselves, value ourselves enough to feel okay with our not okayness. It's the I'm not okay and your not okay, but it's okay theme.

Developmentally, I can see I've made progress. I had dinner in Boston with Bob, a friend who works at American Express. I've done a bunch work with Bob, and we know each other well. Boston is a nice town and has some great seafood places. I checked into the Copley Plaza Hotel. It's a nice old hotel, but a little stodgy. I wore some colorful, baggy pants on the plane ride from Kansas City, my home, to Boston. It's great to wear fun clothes. You're sitting on the plane and somebody looks at you and says, "What do you do?" And I say, "I'm a doctor." It's great.

Then I think, when we go out to dinner, perhaps they'll have a dress code. I don't want to embarrass Bob. I started to change my clothes and then I thought, "No, we'll go out and eat some place where I won't have to worry about that. Bob's not going to care. He'll be totally fine with what I wear." But I went through this scenario in my own mind about what is going to be proper.

It does become a little different when you include other people in the equation. It's one thing to put yourself out there. It's another thing to put someone who's not ready to feel uncomfortable in that way, on the spot. It's somewhat disrespectful to them. So I have sensitivity about that, but I'm probably less concerned about it than I used to be. I see that I have more freedom than I used to in terms of making those kinds of choices. Does that I mean I don't care how I look? Well, not exactly. It's not that I don't care how I look. But, I do have a choice. And, I go for the fun clothes much more frequently.

We can change our expectations. There's a wonderful book called *The Comedy of Survival*, written by Joe Meeker. Joe Meeker has a Ph. D. in comparative literature, and has also been a forest ranger. He's a very interesting person. His book is really about normal not being healthy. He says that our ethical system comes from a culture that has a tragic ethos, a Greek, Hebraic, Christian tragic ethos.

In a tragedy there are very lofty ideals and a lot of people dead at the end of the play. What we can do is change from a tragic ethos to a comedic ethos and downsize our expectations a little bit. A lot of life is about walking around, bumping into things, and trying to learn stuff, while having a few laughs along the way. I think he makes a good point. But, again, it's hard to do what's healthy when we're feeling stressed. We don't access that comedic energy. Our belief system may be, "Well that shouldn't have happened!" Why not?

Perhaps our expectations need to be downsized. There are people who do therapy called cognitive restructuring. Do you know what that's about? Changing your belief system. The therapist says, "What do you mean it *shouldn't* happen?" The client responds, "Well, it shouldn't have happened; it wasn't fair." Therapist: "Well, okay, is life fair?"

If you're waiting around for life to get fair, it may be a long wait. That's an irrational use of the word "should." Pay attention to you—what *you* do, not what other people *should* do.

Aren't we funny how we'll give away power and control to allow some dysfunctional person to drive our behavior and mood. But what was our belief

74

system growing up? A bad apple can spoil the whole bunch. We are not apples. But that's what we tend to do around people who are rotten. And we allow them to infect us with the quality of the energy that they carry, so we need to vaccinate ourselves.

Downsize our expectations and have a few more laughs along the way. Our feelings may allow us to see that we need a booster. What can I do to move in a more positive response direction? Right now, maybe I don't want to talk to that person. Right now, she wants to talk to me, but you know, I don't think I want to talk to her now. "I don't think it's a good idea for me to visit with you right now. I need to sort out my thoughts. I'm confused at the moment and I'm not sure what's going on."

Is it okay to be confused? Is it okay to not know the exact right perfect thing to do? What kind of belief system do we have about that? With a comedic ethos, I can be confused without being embarrassed.

We're supposed to know. But, when we downsize expectations, we give ourselves permission to be confused. It's a wonderful stress management tool. I guarantee it.

As a physician, when someone comes in with a problem, you are supposed to know the exact right perfect thing to do. But, when practicing medicine, guess what? People came in and I didn't know what the hell to do with them. Then I recognized this: people are different, everything isn't a classic textbook example. Things can be confusing and I needed to give myself permission to be confused. Then I could ask colleagues for their opinions, and I could beopen to learning something new. Whereas, when I'm sure I'm right, I'm stuck with what I already know.

Eric Hoffer said, "In times of change, it's the learners who inherit the earth, while the learned find themselves beautifully equipped to deal with a world that no longer exists." Giving ourselves permission to be confused leaves us open to new learning.

Speaking of a comedic ethos, here's an example of normal not being healthy. We wait for Barry to blow germs all over the room and we say "God bless you, Barry." When else do we bless people?

When they die. When we say our prayers. When they're baptized.

In ordinary, everyday conversation,when else do we bless people?

When we sneeze.

That's about it. In my every day, walking-around life, I don't hear people blessing each other a lot. And it's just kind of funny to me that we wait for the sneeze. "Sneeze or Cough? Cough? Sorry I almost blessed you by accident there."

The idea of moving in a more positive response direction may mean I need to get into a psychological space to do it. But just moving into neutral for a while might be useful. The psychological position that may not be normal but might be healthy is to say, "In my life, in my stressful life, who is THE with a capital T, problem? Other people? My ex? My kids? My coworkers? My boss? Who is thee capital T, problem? Me. I am the problem.

Are we used to seeing our leaders stand up and say, "I am the problem." Did Richard Nixon stand up and say "I am the problem." Or Bill Clinton say, "I am the problem." No. We're used to people blaming other people: republicans blame democrats, democrats blame republicans, conservatives blame liberals,

liberals blame conservatives. If only they would change, everything would be better. And in our marriages, "If only they would change, everything would be better." In our relationships with other people, "If only they changed..."

STOP. THEY ARE NOT THE PROBLEM. I AM. But if I am the problem in my life, what else am I?

The solution. Indeed.

Ah! This is a key piece. If I'm I problem in my life—Capital T—I'm also the solution. What are the things that I could do to be healthy and have healthy relationships with other people without them changing, how can I be more effective at what I do and have more fun getting better?

Those things interest me. Including the performance piece. How can I get better at what I do? Because my bias is that I am an underachiever and so are you. Relative to what we're capable of doing, in terms of expressing our giftedness, everyone's an underachiever. The funny thing is, it may be our stressful life events that stimulate us to move to the next level of performance. Remember Rat #1? We can't reach peak performance without being stressed.

Have you ever gotten a promotion and felt more stress? You were doing something well and bang, what happened? The boss walks in and gives you a promotion. Shit. Now you have more responsibilities. But that's good stress. Our stressors can be good (eustress) or bad (distress) that generate our negative responses.

If I'm the problem, I'm also the solution. That means I'm going to focus my flashlight on what's on my plate and eat it. The boss puts a new job on my plate. How can I best adapt to this new INput and be a healthy variation as a leader? What leadership traits of former bosses would I like to model? Whom shall I ask to mentor me in this new job? I can get the group of people that I now lead and serve together and ask them how I could best support them.

It will feel a little awkward; they were my peers. I think I'll tell them that I feel awkward and ask them to bear with me as I figure out how to do something I haven't done before. With their help, I think I'll eventually catch on. I think I'll use that "slow but trainable line. Yeah, that's the ticket. "

"I'm happy to have this new stress in my life but I'm confused about how to best do this job. I will figure it out. But I need your help. I have, as we all do, a small brain. But, together we have a big brain. Work with me and I'll finally get it. Remember, I'm slow but trainable. I will eventually catch on."

In relationships with other people, wouldn't we rather nibble on their plate? It's a metaphor. With our own children don't we have permission to eat off our kid's plate? "I bought the food, let me taste it." In a metaphorical sense, that's what we do. We nibble off of each other's plate. If I eat what's on my own plate what might I have to do? Eat my own stuff.

Eating what's on my own plate might create some fullness, some indigestion, and make me uncomfortable. I might not like it. Why? Because then I might have to change.

Exactly! We don't like it as much as eating off somebody else's plate. But if I do that, what it really means, in my stressful life I'm focusing on me using my life events as fuel for growth.

And if I eat it, then I may have to change my behavior and my responses to life. But if we give ourselves permission to be confused as we learn to do what we do better, who knows, we might even have fun in the process.

The wonderful thing about us, the thing that makes us unique amongst all animals, is the ability to change. But, it's very stressful! It's less stressful, in some ways, to try to manipulate or control somebody else to change. Owning our own stuff is stressful. Being the problem in our life is stressful. In some ways it is less stressful to play the role of victim and to blame the people who were in our environment when we were growing up.

But maybe our stressful events, maybe the unfairness of life, can serve us developmentally by helping us grow and mature into what we potentially are. Instead of simply doing what the grownups who came before us did, we can break the cycle. That's one of the reasons why I like to talk about why normal isn't healthy. Because a lot of people who don't have overt, obvious dysfunction themselves or in the family, think they're doing all right and don't need to change.

CHAPTER 8

THE MAKING OF OUR BEST-KEPT SECRET

If I'm going to respond in new ways to my life without INput changing, is it going to be easy? No. If someone says it's going to be easy, it's a con. It's not easy. It's hard. It's easier to do what we already know, even if it doesn't work. It is easier to take the path of least resistance.

What makes it worse is this: When I quit doing what's predictable, when I quit giving away power and control to other people, when I accept responsibility for my own situation and begin to work on changing me, other people who in the past have been able to manipulate me into predictable patterns of response, are not going to give me support for my new behaviors. In fact they may say, "I think he's gone over the edge."

That's the irony. We're doing something that's healthier, and people, even people in our own family, may say, "What's wrong with you?" The old support system collapses. In may not be there in the way that it was in the past. But we need healthy support. For me to have the courage to change, for me to have the courage to face my own stuff and to quit blaming others, I need encouragement.

I need other nuts in my support system. Because when I'm doing something that I don't know how to do, guess what I'm going to do a few times, perhaps over and over? Make mistakes. I'm going to fall on my face. And when I fall on my face, because that's so humiliating, I may go back to my old ways of reacting to INput.

It's uncomfortable to be so vulnerable. Getting through that is difficult. It is doubly so because as a belief system, did we hear it was a good idea to be vulnerable when growing up?

No.

Have you ever played team sports? Did you ever hear the coach at half time say, "Okay now team, I want you to go out there and be vulnerable." I don't remember that half-time talk. Being vulnerable is very awkward for most of us and that's why we need support.

THE EARLY YEARS

I've been talking about this movie business. Let's tie it into the whole idea of support and relationships. I use the analogy that life is a movie because it's a simple model with which everybody is familiar. We've all gone to a movie, and seen the beginning, the middle, and the end. We know there's a story that unfolds during the movie. The movie is a way to tell a story. And everybody is logical in the context of the movie of their life.

We may hear a story about a man who beats his wife and have a hard time believing that someone is capable of being violent with someone they claim to love. We want to judge this man. We want to think this man should have never been born. But no one is a mistake or an accident. The problem is that in our relationships we walk into the middle of each other's movies. We don't know why other people are so screwed up because we haven't seen them in the context of their own development.

It would be like going to a movie complex early, getting your treats, sitting down, and thinking you've walked into the previews when you're actually in the middle of a movie because you are in the wrong theater. You're

81

early because you always get there early so, you watch five minutes of the movie and then you go in and see the movie you came to see.

Within the five-minute snipet, you see this character with this obvious flaw. You think, what a schmuck, you have no sympathy or compassion for the character because he's such a creep. And then it's time to go see the movie you came to see. Two weeks later you go back to the complex. You see that movie from the beginning. When you come to the five-minute piece you saw before, you see the character flaw in the context of the storyline and you have sympathy and compassion for the character. You can even identify with the character because you have understanding.

We can't rewind our movies to the beginning and move forward frame-by-frame. Psychoanalysis is really about that process. People might spend an hour a day, five days a week, for ten years trying to unwind the movie. For most of us, that is probably unnecessary. I don't think we have to do that.

I think we also need to honor the fact that if we rewound all our movies and pushed "play" there'd be lots of differences among us. But, as you have noticed, what I want to talk about are the things we share in common, regardless of the differences. One thing we share in common is that we all begin our movie the same way.

We begin our lives in a dependent state. We're born totally dependent. We're dependent in the womb for what? Nine months? During the end of that period, there's a lot of growth in the brain, the organ of learning. There's evidence to show that in the womb, there's audio and then when we're born, we enter the womb with a view. We pick up the video piece.

I say womb with a view because the world the newborn inhabits is like an external womb. We are semimarsupial in that the local environment of the neonate is similar to the marsupial pouch. In infancy, we are just as dependent upon the mother or mothering figure as the fetus is. At birth, he information we absorbed in utero, the tonal quality and the stress present in the voices of people in the environment, now has a visual component. Once the child is born there may be an association with learning that began in utero and continues after birth.

Regardless, the whole idea is that the dependent state we inhabited in the womb continues long after birth. In fact, we have the longest period of dependency of any animal upon parents or parental figures. We're not like the wildebeest. We can't run with the herd an hour after birth. It takes us a couple of decades to be able to run with the grownups.

We're not adequate to take care of ourselves in the jungle that is the world. So, we all start out the movie of our lives playing a dependent role. Regardless of our cultural or ethnic differences, we share this in common.

We are born with our gaze outward turned. Scientists know for sure that as soon as we're born, the brain is active and absorbing information. Our brains are sponges and our absorbent minds are taking in, by osmosis, what is going on around us.

We look into the field of action. If life is a movie, we begin to live our lives in reference to our producers: the giants, the magical beings; the ones who could walk, talk, move all their parts, carry us around, and feed us . . . our parents. It's in this dependent relationship to the parents that we begin the first reel of the movie of our lives, and begin to learn about self and world.

One of the implications of this long period of dependency, i.e., not being adequate to take care of ourselves, is that every little kid will have feelings of inadequacy. Every toddler, preschooler and grade-schooler will have feelings of inadequacy and insecurity. When do those feelings go away?

Do they go away when we graduate from high school or get that college degree? Do they go away when we finish graduate school and get our Ph.D., M.D., J.D., or L.L. Bean? Do they go away if we become parents? When we're in our thirties, in our forties, or if we become grandparents? Do they go away when we go into management or become the head Fred of the company?

Our feelings of inadequacy never go away, but it's like a secret that we share that we don't talk about. So we walk around acting like we know what we're doing. Doctors are particularly good at it. We went to school forever and we have special initials up there in front of the name. At the doctor's lounge at the hospital where I go do you think the doctors sit around talking about their feelings of inadequacy?

"Hi, refer your patients to me, I'm inadequate" doesn't get you a lot of referrals.

My father was a doctor and when we would go to a restaurant as a family, what name would he leave with the hostess? Doctor White. Why would he say doctor? Was that who he was, or was that what he did? Part of normal not being healthy is that we get them mixed up. We often confuse what we do for who we are.

Now, why don't those feelings of inadequacy ever go away?

Because they are woven into the fabric of the psyche very early in our development when we were open and unconsciously absorbing INput. How?

Use your own database of life experience. How do we show how adequate we are in our role as parents? The performance of our children shows the world what kind of job we're doing as parents. So, we shine the flashlight of our attention on our children's behavior. We put their behavior under a microscope.

As a result, the behavior of the child takes on a magnified importance relative to the relationship with the parental figure. The parent, to compensate for their own feelings of inadequacy, wants to put their best foot, rather child, forward.

Do you have these bumper stickers in your community? The ones that read:

PROUD PARENT OF HONOR ROLE STUDENT AT MAPLE WOOD SCHOOL.

I'm an adequate parent. Thank you very much. Just wanted to make sure you knew it, so I put it on the car.

Have you seen the joke on those?

MY KID BEAT UP YOUR HONOR ROLE STUDENT.

I'm adequate too, buddy.

But you don't see bumper stickers like this:

PROUD PARENT. REGARDLESS OF THEIR GRADES

MY KIDS HAVE AN A IN MY BOOK.

Why don't we see bumper stickers like that? Could it be that what we're talking about is a secret that we share that we don't talk about? I think one of the reasons we ought to talk about it is this: If our children think we're only proud of them when they do things right or do things well, then there's a huge "if" clause in the relationship.

"If" you make your grades, I'm proud to be your dad. "If" you make your grades I'm proud to be your mom. "If" you clean you room, "if" you clean the kitchen, whatever.

In my relationships with my four daughters, I don't want there to be an "if" clause. It's not, "if" you do something well, I'm proud to be your dad. It's, regardless of what you do, I'm so lucky to be your dad. You are a treasure in my life. Not because you do something right, or you do something well but just because you're you—you are a treasure. I'm so thankful. Everyday I thank God for my children. Everyday I ask them, "Have I told you today how wonderful you are? Have I told you today, that you have an "A" in my book?"

If there is an "if" clause in my relationship with my children, then I may only hear about their successes. When things are going well, I want to know. But, when they really need my healthy support is when things are not going so well, when they are having a hard time. I want them to know they can come to me with their worst failures and that I will be there as a member of their circle of support.

Now, when we were little kids growing up, somebody forgot to look us right in the eye and tell us what a treasure we were. Not because we did something right or we did something well. Not because of how we performed on the world stage. Not just when they caught us being good or a perfect little gentleman/lady . . . not anything related to how we looked or to some task-specific behavior.

We did get messages. We heard and absorbed many messages over and over. Early on, no one minds if we poop in our pants, spit out our food, dribble when we vocalize, or even pee on someone. But, over time, that all changes. We learn there are right and wrong ways of doing things.

We don't start out the movie of our life knowing the rules. But, we soon learn, regardless of cultural or ethnic differences, that "there's only one way of doing things and that's the right way. Anything worth doing, is worth doing right. If you can't do it well, don't do it at all. And if you really want it done right, do it yourself."

Right! And what do parents do when children do things wrong? We correct them, of course. Now does this radiant little child learn to do things right upon the first correction? Of course not. Children, like adults, need repetition, repetition, repetition to learn most things.

And we've all heard, "If I've told you once I've told you a thousand times to chew with your mouth closed. Do you have a hearing problem? Do we need to clean out those ears? When we parked the car to walk in here, did your brain fall out? Do we have to go find your brain and put your brain back in your head?"

I'll give you an example. Let's say Barry's my son. He's my five-year-old son, and we've just been to religious services. He's got his little sincere suit on and, after services, there's a little supper. And he's eating in such a fashion that food is falling out of his face. He is goobering his sincere suit because he's chewing with his mouth open. Now, as Barry's parent, what is it my job to do?

Correct him. It's not rocket science.

"Barry, would you please chew with your mouth shut." Now, Barry's a bright boy, but is he going to learn the first time he's taught? No! We need repetition, repetition, repetition. "Barry, if I've told you once, I've told you a thousand times, chew with your mouth shut."

"Gee, a thousand times. If he's told me a thousand times, I really am stupid," thinks Barry.

Now, as Barry's father, it's not that I woke up that morning thinking, "You know, I think I'll give little Barry a religious experience this morning." I didn't wake up planning to reinforce little Barry's feelings of inadequacy today. But because what we're talking about is a secret that we share that we don't talk about, I do what was done with me. I carry my culture like a baton and pass it to the next generation.

"So, I turned out all right, didn't I? It's what my dad did with me."

Is that our function as parents, to simply replicate the behaviors of those who raised us without questioning? Just because something works, doesn't mean it's a good idea.

"Look, when my son does something wrong, it is my job to discipline him, to correct him."

Exactly. Spare the rod; spoil the child. Correct him. And the baton moves from father to son.

"Listen here, it's not just that he is a reflection on me and the whole family. He needs to learn the social amenities, so he doesn't create resistance in a social milieu."

Grandparents come and visit their kids and their grandchildren. And the grandparents let the grandkids do stuff they never let the parents do when they were kids. And the parents say, "Well you never let us do that when we were kids!"

"Well of course I didn't! I didn't know what I was doing!"

People should actually be grandparents before they're parents because grandparents are much less obsessed with some of the things we become obsessed with as parents. One of the reasons we're so concerned with the behavior of our children is that the behavior of our children reveals to the world what kind of job we're doing in our role as parents.

Eventually, we learned the socially acceptable behavior sets. When we performed the right behavior, perhaps someone even caught us being good, once. "Your mother and I are very proud to see you're chewing with your mouth closed." Having learned that behavior, they could then focus on another flaw!

Our feelings of inadequacy keep getting reinforced by parents, coaches, teachers, peers, siblings, scout leaders, clergy. Of course, with clergy, we don't have to actually make a mistake. We don't have to actually do anything wrong. Thinking it is the same as doing it, and whether or not we've ever done it, we've all thought about it.

So, growing up, in the process of learning the right way to do things, we all received much more specific negative feedback than specific positive feedback. And because what we're discussing is a secret that we share that we don't talk about, our feelings of inadequacy were reinforced more often than the good feelings we carried.

And when we were affirmed, it was related to task-specific behavior. The "when," was connected to an "if": "If" you do something well, "then" you get my good stuff, my warmth.

Do you see how this is related to learning how to get emotional food from the giants we are dependent upon in the first reel of the movie? It is a symbiotic relationship. The behavior of the child demonstrates the adequacy of the parent. The child pleases the parent and in return gets an emotional "fix" in the form of warmth and praise. It feels good getting the affirmation from the parent. So, the child, or at least the compliant child, goes for what feels good. The child figures out how to please the parent.

In giving a pleasing performance for others, the child compensates for feelings of inadequacy. The "A" on the grade card shows that the child is "A" for adequate. And everyone is pleased.

The same dynamic is reinforced later in life when the child is accepted to the Ivy League school, to grad school, law school, med school, it's all the same. If our child got accepted to Stanford, would we put a sticker on the car or figure out some other more subtle way of bringing this adequacy into the flashlight of someone's attention?

If the child can't please the parent, or doesn't feel that he can, he will find someone he can please, someone who will accept him as adequate. Perhaps it's a gang member with whom the child moves into a compliant relationship. Now, the strength of the gang is great psychic compensation for feelings of inadequacy. They have their own symbols to let others know of their social status.

Because this is a secret that we share that we don't talk about, when children make mistakes the grownups end up reinforcing their own kids' feelings of inadequacy. It's not something we're doing consciously. We don't wake up in the morning thinking, "I think I'll reinforce Tracy's feelings of inadequacy," but we end up doing that simply because we all carry culture and we pass culture on from generation to generation. We do what was modeled to us by the grownups who came before us. Now we are them. We are the people we used to complain about, and it's time for us to break the cycle.

We break the cycle by starting with us. Do not bother with the blame game. That's not going to be particularly productive. The grownups around us when we were kids did the best job they could with the information they had about how to do grownup. If you could run all of their movies backward and then advance frame-by-frame, you'd see the exquisite logic of their behavior. They couldn't have done anything differently. If this is a secret we share, and we don't talk about it now, they certainly didn't talk about it when we were little kids.

We know that we don't start out knowing the right way to do stuff. We have to learn. There are different learning styles: visual, auditory, kinesthetic.

But what's the final common pathway of learning? Experience. You see somebody do something, then you try it yourself. Are you going to do it right the first time? Most likely not. What's required for learning? Practice. Why? Because we earn our learning the old fashion way, one mistake at a time.

The final common pathway of learning is mistake making. We learn by trial and error. But, in the process of learning the right way, to do anything, we make mistakes. We eventually learn the right way to do things. You don't dump in your shorts anymore, do you?

I hope not.

91

When we start the movie of our life, we don't know anything, let alone the right way to do things. We have to learn everything. We all learn how to do a lot of things really well. But how do we learn to feel about ourselves? You get to see how you feel about yourself when you make a mistake. When you make a mistake, are you kind, compassionate, gentle, and forgiving? Hardly.

How were we taught to feel when we made a mistake? In fact, what was the right way to feel when we make mistakes?

Ashamed, "Aren't you ashamed of yourself?"

That's right. "Bad boy, get your hands off your brother!

"That's a bad girl. Don't ever let me see you do that again!"

"Barry! Get your hands off yourself, we're in church for Pete's sake. I told you no digging in church."

So, it isn't just that we make mistakes. We should be punished, reprimanded. So, we beat ourselves up. We are supposed to feel bad when we screw up, and we learn to focus our flashlight on the mistake.

We don't focus on what we are learning, instead we feel bad about ourselves. We learned the right way to do stuff but that doesn't mean we learned to feel great about who we are. Although we might feel good about something that we do for a couple of seconds, we can't seem to sustain the feeling because there's the next thing. And the next thing, and the bar goes up.

Did we start out feeling bad when we made mistakes? No! Kids pretty much stay where you put them until about four months. You have your baby in the bassinet in the living room and they're two months old, you can be pretty sure he'll be there when you come back in a couple of minutes. But at about four months babies begin to roll over. A few months later they are crawling around.

92

After several months, your baby crawls over to something and pulls himself up. He holds on to steady himself but is courageous and, by golly, lets go. And what happens? He falls down. Now what does he do?

"Ah shit, I can't believe I can't walk yet. Little Jimmy is twelve months old and he's walking all over the place—look at me! What the hell's wrong with me?"

No! He crawls back over, pulls himself back up, tries again, falls down, gets back up, lets go again.

Children are irrepressible learners, trying over and over to walk. Did that feel bad? No. In fact, it was an adventure in learning. Children are out exploring their world.

But, over time, we don't explore so much anymore. We've inhaled too much negative reinforcement. We get it everywhere. Because what we're talking about is a secret that we share that we don't talk about, when children make mistakes, we end up reinforcing their feelings of inadequacy.

The acculturation process is the same for all of us, regardless of cultural variances. The differences are small because it doesn't matter what the culture is. In any culture, there is a right way "to do" things.

Children don't know the right way to do things. So we school them. And the schooling is both formal and informal. We learn the right ways to do things but the wrong way to feel about ourselves. We can then feel good about what we do but bad about who we are.

Some primitive cultures honor the child and the process of the child's development. The children are allowed to push culture. The new things that the children do that the older generation didn't, are inculcated into the culture—into the dances, into the tradition. The adults watch the children and see what the children bring from the other world.

NEOTENY

Ashley Montagu writes about development in his wonderful book *Growing Young*. Montagu says that we're not meant to grow up into the kinds of adults that we become; we're not meant to grow old, we're meant to grow young. What he is says is supported by the fossil record; it's supported by evolution theory. I'll show you a wonderful visual.

(pictures of adolescent and adult chimp)

Look at the picture of a juvenile chimp. What's it look like? It looks like a human child except for the big ears and some extra hair. Look at the adult chimp. More hair, but what else? What happened to that flat face? It grew out. The flat face is gone.

The immature trait of the juvenile chimp is not sustained throughout development. The flat face is gone. Now this big mandible juts out forward. Why? The chimp does not sustain the juvenile trait throughout development. But we do. You look at a child in profile--flat face; adult—flat face. We hold on to the immature traits throughout development. We are neotenous.

In *Growing Young*, Montagu wrote about neoteny. Neoteny is a great word, but not a word you hear in everyday conversations, not yet. It's a fun word and a better concept. We are the most neotenous of all animals. It's a reference to the fact that we retain immature physical traits into adulthood.

Another word for neoteny is pedomorphism. Pedo—meaning pediatric, child. Morphism meaning morphology, or shape. What evolutionary intelligence is showing us is that we're supposed to maintain the shape, the morphology, of the child throughout development—pedomorphism.

Neoteny says we are meant to hold onto the physical traits of the child throughout development. Montagu, as a cultural anthropologist, argues that we are meant to hold onto the behavioral traits as well.

We're not meant to grow old. We're meant to grow young, to stay in a developmental process our whole lives. All those wonderful behavioral traits of the child--plasticity, authenticity, playfulness, spontaneity, laughter, tears, experimental mindedness--are meant to be sustained throughout the life cycle. But what happens?

We learn how to do things right, how to do things well, thereby, establishing that we're adequate in the eyes of other people. And then we keep doing what we already know how to do, that in which we've already established adequacy. Why? Because the part of us that has feelings of inadequacy feels safe doing what we already know how to do.

How does that part of us that has those feelings of inadequacy feel about change? How does that part of us feel about learning something new? About exploring new ground? Scared! Exactly! Because what's required for learning?

Mistakes.

And when I make a mistake how may you see me?

As inadequate.

So how can I stay safe?

By not trying anything new.

Don't change. Don't learn. Keep doing what I already know how to do. Don't develop. We compensate for what's unresolved within the psyche by how we act on the world stage.

In some respect, to compensate for my feelings of inadequacy, I became a physician. All of the training in medical school is about what's wrong with other people. We don't have one day on what's wrong with us. It's a little unbalanced. As a doctor you get a special outfit, you get to use special initials in your name, have special status in certain circles. But inside, every physician is carrying a secret.

CHAPTER 9

THE SCARED ONE

The scared one. I call the part of me that has those feelings of inadequacy "the scared one." All of us have a scared one inside of us. But it's like a secret that we share that we don't talk about. So we walk around acting like we know what we're doing. We learned it from the grownups. Now, we're the people we used to complain about. We are them. We're the grownups.

It's really important to talk about this secret because it connects back to how we do support, to how we do relationships. It connects back to performance issues. It connects back to learning. It connects at a core level of the psyche to almost everything humans do.

This part of me, the scared one, gets in the way of me fully unfolding my giftedness. Because once I've established that I can do something adequately, I keep doing what I know. This part of me then feels safe, because in the eyes of other people I can do what I know adequately. The motto of the scared one is safety and security at all costs.

Is the scared one equal to the ego? Is it one and the same? Good question. They are both interested in survival. But I don't think you can have a healthy scared one, although you can have a healthy ego. I think the scared one is an aspect of the ego, but I don't think it's the same thing. Is it anything like an inner child? I don't see it that way. An inner child can be healthy. An inner child can feel radiant.

To break out of my familiar behaviors—to break out of doing what I know, to try something new, to do something I haven't done before—well now, it's scary. To a little kid it isn't. Novelty is engaging. It's interesting. The child's motto is, go for it. Run, don't walk, leap and skip into every day . . . until we grow up a little.

Talking about our best-kept secret is important for many reasons, starting with our relationship to ourselves. At this stage of our life, as grownups, do we need anyone else to reinforce our feelings of inadequacy? No. We do a good enough job all by ourselves, thank you.

Part of normal not being healthy is that we learn to be our own worst enemy. When was the last time you heard someone say, "Yeah, I'm my own best friend!"

What's your own self-talk like when you screw up and don't meet your own expectations? Are you kind, benevolent, gentle, or . . . ?

For some folks, it depends on whether it's in private or public. Some people feel obligated to be ashamed and embarrassed if they make a mistake in front of other people.

Alex, a bright thirty-eight-year-old woman, recently said to a group of us, "If you don't berate yourself, it means you don't really care. Because if you really cared, you'd feel like a piece of shit right now.

"There is a little kid I know. I went over to his house on his birthday. I didn't give him a birthday present, that day, because what I got him for Christmas he didn't like. So I was going to talk to him about what he wanted. So I show up, and he immediately goes, 'Alex, where's my birthday present?' And his mother says, 'Joey!' and gets mad at him.

"She's usually super patient and loving and everything. But I go, 'That's okay, it's his birthday. He wants to know where his birthday present is.' But to her—we talked about it later—it would be rude of her not to get mad at him. It's crazy."

But, it's absolutely logical. We are concerned with our image in the eyes of other people, because the scared one is really concerned about being exposed as inadequate. So we want to project images to other people to compensate. We want to be seen as adequate, or even better, superior. Her child's behavior was a reflection on her. She didn't want Alex to think she didn't care or that she wasn't a good mother.

Is it crazy? No, it's logical, and it's normal for parents to correct their children in public to show that they care. That's just a good example of something less than sound thinking.

The mother doesn't know what to do except to go back to how her mother would react and does what her mom did with her.

Those types of parenting messages are so present in the psyche. There's a momentum that's never lost. I can go back into that psychological space instantaneously.

My dad has been dead since October 13, 1993, but who's counting? I didn't take my kids over to my parent's house too often because my father, whom I loved dearly, was somewhat controlling. I didn't really want my kids around him that much because of some of what we have been talking about here.

Early one morning, however, I went over to visit my folks. I took one of our girls, who was crawling around on the floor with the dog. I was not paying that much attention and all of a sudden I hear this booming voice, "Bad dog!"

I felt a bolt of lightening go through my body when I heard that. And what do you think I flashed on? "Bad boy!" The same booming voice I'd heard decades earlier yelling at me was so present. It was as if there was no gap between hearing the voice and the memory. It was an electrical shock in my body.

I don't blame my dad. He was doing the best job he could do with the information he got about how to do grownup. But, I sure don't want to do that with my children.

There's a wonderful scene in *Regarding Henry*. Did you see *Regarding Henry*? It's a movie with a Park Avenue attorney played by Harrison Ford, who is married to a beautiful woman played by Annette Bening. They have a wonderful daughter and a fairytale Park Avenue life. Ford's character goes down to get cigarettes at one of those mom and pop groceries in New York City. When he goes into the grocery, there is a robbery underway. He says that he just wants cigarettes. But, the gun-toting robber looks at him, aims, and shoots. He hits him in the head.

Ford's character isn't killed. He goes to rehab and has a movie-time recovery of about three weeks. He gets shot in the head, and it affects his memory. He can't remember anything. He's there at the rehab place, making progress, and then it's time for him to go home. Does he want to leave? No. He knows that place. It's familiar ,and he doesn't know the other one, his home. And get this: He's shot in the head, his memory's gone, but what does he still have?

A scared one. A scared one who wants to stay safe.

He wants to stay in rehab with the attendant who has cared for him. He doesn't want to go home. But he does. He goes home and has to reinvent himself. He has to learn about what he was like. He learns he was a total creep. He was an unethical attorney. He was having an affair. He didn't like what he learned about himself.

The scenes in the movie with he and his daughter are so beautiful. His daughter is his mentor and teaches him to read. That's a switch. There's a scene in the movie where the family is having a meal together, and the daughter knocks over her drink. She spills her drink and looks up at her dad. And he says, "That's okay." He knocks his drink over, "I do it all the time." I thought that was great. In how many homes in America, when a child accidentally knocks over a glass of milk, does the parent go (splash) "that's okay I do it all the time"?

Do we have to be shot in the head? No, but sometimes it seems like it. If we don't scold our children, what may happen? They'll never learn to drink without spilling. Do you think scolding helps a lot? And it's such a serious thing isn't it? Oh my God, I can't believe you spilled your drink. What's wrong with you!? It's a serious thing.

We magnify stuff that's not important and allow it to distract us from infusing our love and warmth into our children. But this is our experience, our communal experience. And we've got it down pat. We know how to do grownup. We know how to do things right. We know how to do things well.

But we can be doing the best job we can with the information we received about doing grownup and not know how to be healthy. We know how to do grownup but do not know how to have healthy, coequal, non-controlling, loving, affectionate relationships. And I think the central, the core piece of that problem is connected to how we learn to feel about ourselves.

My treatment of my four daughters has nothing to do with how I feel about them. How I treat them is about how I feel about me. I love them dearly, but they don't always get my best juice. And it doesn't have anything to do with them.

When I'm feeling good about me, accepting of me *with* my flaws, hang-ups, and neuroses, I treat my children well. When I don't have an "if" clause in my relationship with myself, when I give myself permission to own my humanity, my clay-footed nature, then I'm meek, tolerant, and patient with them. When I'm not feeling so good about me, when I'm on automatic pilot—running around doing my important grownup stuff with never enough time to get everything done—I can revert back and do what my dad did with me.

Developmentally I can see I've made progress. I use the number twenty-nine. I think I'm awake about 29 percent of the time in terms of being healthy instead of normal. It used to be 28 percent of the time. I see I've made a modicum of change. I'm moving in the direction of being awake more and therefore healthy more. But I can still access all that old material instantaneously. I can shame my own children in a heartbeat. I'll give you an example.

In addition to being a physician, I travel the planet sharing my confusion with others at conferences and workshops and consulting with those foolish enough to risk inflicting me upon their organization. So, I travel a lot. I came home one Friday night feeling guilty about not having been home for several days. So, I figure out a game plan to assuage my guilt.

Tomorrow morning I'm going to wake up with Brynn and Jordan, the youngest two, who were four and seven at the time. I'll get up with them and fix breakfast. I'll goof around with them and keep them out of the older kids' room and my wife's hair. So when the three of them come down late Saturday morning, they will see what a great father and husband I am.

So I get up early the next morning with Brynn and Jordan, feed them breakfast, and then we go into the living room. They start goofing around, playing together, and having fun. I pick up the paper and begin to read. The plan is working great. Then all of a sudden, they start to kill each other. You know what I mean, if you're a parent. It doesn't take long.

If you've seen kids, they can turn in a heartbeat. All of a sudden they're making all this noise. What's my thought? *They're going to ruin my plan. Wait a second here!* So I say, "You're obviously having trouble playing together. So here's the deal—play separately for a while and then after you cool down, you can play together again." Now, as I'm saying this, the four year old, Jordan, marches over, picks up a bucket of Brynn's toys, dumps it on the ground, and marches back to her place.

"Hey Jordan, it's one thing to spill something by accident, but what you just did, you did on purpose. So here's the deal—you can play anytime you want, after you choose to pick up the stuff that you spilled." Pretty hip parenting, don't you think? But then I had to add the caboose. Ever do this? "Jordan you can play anytime you want after you choose to pick up the stuff that you spilled, *so why don't you pick it up now?*" Remember the inverse relationship between control and motivation? "Why don't you pick it up now?" creates resistance.

So Jordan is totally defiant. She stands there with her arms folded, chin up, and looking in the opposite direction of Brynn. You ever do this one? If our children are defiant, in what do we invest energy? Having to win. I mean, who's in charge here anyway? "Jordan did you hear me? I said get over there and pick up Brynn's stuff."

The scared one has an evil twin. Big one. The big one's got a big voice and likes to have things happen at his pace. Keep in mind that in my mind I had established that the last thing I was going to do was parent like my dad. I'd make a mistake and my dad would say, "Go get the hairbrush!" Do you think I'm going to go get the hairbrush? Actually this is what he'd say first. "Do you want a good hard spanking?" What kind of question is that? Yes, no, yes, no . . .

Regardless, mvoice is getting bigger, and I hear myself saying, "Jordan get over there and pick that up NOW!" Do you know what her response was? Do you think she ran right over and picked up? No, she looks me in the eye and gives me the bird. She gave me the finger! I totally freaked. I picked her up, carried her in the other room, and put her underneath the dining room table. We don't spank in our family. We can shame our children in other ways.

As I'm justifying my big one's treatment of my child, I thought, "If I gave my dad the finger, I would not have the finger!" I was abrupt with her, you know, and I'm thinking, "Man I just can't believe it." Then there's this voice inside my head. The voice starts to say, *Gee, she's only four years old. I wonder if she knows what that means.*

Do you think I want to hear that voice? No, I do not want to hear that voice. I am justifying my actions but this voice keeps saying, *She's only four years old. She probably doesn't know what that means.* She probably didn't know what it means. She probably saw it in the neighborhood or on TV and probably didn't know what it means. But I showed her that it's a very powerful hand signal!

I realized that I had just screwed up again. I go in the other room and crawl underneath the table. Jordan's sitting there sucking her thumb, clutching her blankee, and holding back this wall of tears. I say, "Jordan, do you know what it means?" while I displayed the prominent third digit. And she shook her head. She didn't know what it means.

I said, "I'm so sorry Jordan. Someday I'll explain to you what it means. It's not nice. I'm so sorry I over reacted. I love you so much." With that she pulls her thumb out of her mouth, puts her arms around me, and this wall of tears comes down her face. I'm sitting there, and tears are coming down my face as we slobber on each other underneath the table. Because what I was doing with her was disrespectful, we both went out together and picked up the toys and put them in the bucket.

Later, I started thinking about my treatment of my daughter. How was I feeling about myself, having been absent for several days? Bad. Guilty. So to compensate for those feelings, I mistreated my daughter. Not because of how I felt about her but because of how I felt about me.

We don't act big and powerfully unless we're feeling small. The bully in school acts big and powerful with the weaker children to compensate for feelings of inadequacy. Domestic violence of men toward women isn't about how men feel about women. It's about how the man feels about himself. Feeling inadequate, weak, in some psychological sense, impotent, he acts out big and powerfully, potently, and in an abusive way.

Well, I think it's time to talk about this secret, that we all have these feelings of inadequacy, because it's connected to all of our relationships. We can't shine the flashlight of our attention on something until we know it's there, until we make overt what's covert. If something is driving behaviors, let's look to see what it is. And in terms of human relationships, I think keeping the secret of the scared one and not talking about what's driving our behavior is a core reason why normal isn't healthy. This isn't part of the public dialog. It isn't part of the discussion, yet.

We never get rid of this part of us. Much of the material wealth in the world is the result of people who are being driven, unconsciously, by their scared one to compensate for their feelings of inadequacy. The irony is that we call that wealth, whereas the original definition of wealth meant "well-being."

Look what we've created here in the United States, the land of opportunity, for people to come from other countries to prove how adequate they are. To live the American dream is a material thing, and the rest of the world is replicating our model. They are looking at us and doing what we do. It is follow the leader, and we are it. Is that all we want to give them?

I don't think so. But, it's time to tell our secrets. It's time to talk about what we haven't been talking about. And this book is simply a little nudge for the sleeping giant who is dreaming the American dream. But it's a little reminder that adds something of value, right now, in our lives. Because it isn't about going somewhere other than where we are. It's about being who we are and where we are with some awareness. With awareness, we can begin to make changes.

Ashley Montagu's definition of health is the ability to work, love, play, and think soundly. What do you think we're good at? Work. We have the working part down pat. How about love and play and think soundly? Let's take love. If the way I treat my children is about how I feel about me, what gets in my way of fully loving them without an "if" clause? Me.

So, the idea is, if I accept that I have this scared part of me, I can pay attention to that part of me and not let it determine my behavior. Without awareness, my scared one can drive the engine of my psyche and pull the rest of

106

me along. And without awareness, I can have the accruements of wealth and not well-being.

SELF-ESTEEM

The idea of having this scared part of me doesn't diminish me. Can I have self-esteem and still have feelings of inadequacy? Yes. I have to be able to accept me as I am and esteem and value myself as I am, not pretend I'm different. Do I have value and worth as I am, with feelings of inadequacy? Yes. Here's the rub. We don't understand self-esteem.

Somebody comes into my office, and I ask, "How's it going?"

"Well, you wouldn't believe it. My self-esteem is in the toilet. I just got laid off."

Did his self-esteem go in the toilet? Or was he really referring to his esteem in the eyes of other people? I mean if you're not a productive member of the community, if you don't have a job, what are you going to say to people when they ask what you do? Did his job loss cause him to lose self-esteem or other esteem? Other esteem. He didn't have self-esteem, or much of it. That's an example of not thinking soundly.

I think self-esteem has nothing to do with doing. It has to do with being. And it's not related to performance or task-specific behavior. I'm not diminished because I make a mistake. But if I don't understand that, I will use my mistake as a reason to reinforce my feelings of inadequacy, giving fuel to the scared one and diminishing self-esteem.

So, going out and doing something right or doing something well feels good. Does the feeling last? No. Then we have the next goal. The bar goes up, and we have the next hurdle to jump over to prove that we have value. It is exhausting to keep chasing the notion that there is a critical mass of other esteem that we can magically convert into self-esteem. That is magical thinking. Self-esteem does not pop out of a hat.

One of the things I've recognized is that I haven't met anybody yet who doesn't have a scared one. That's a broad brush stroke, I know. But if it's there and we all have one, then isn't it a relief to know we are not alone?

But this is what we do in relationships. I compare myself with Frank . He's bright, articulate, self-confident. I compare myself with him, and I'm a schmuck. We take the wonderfulness of other people and see that we don't measure up. We use the wonderfulness of another person to reinforce our own feelings of inadequacy.

What about the not so wonderful? What about the people who have to point out the flaws in everybody else? Gee, I wonder what that's about? Could it be that they are feeling a little inadequate? Is it necessary to point out everybody else's flaws?

The ways we do that are manifold, from crass to creative. Our sub-personalities are all spokes of a wheel. When you get down to the hub, the scared one is giving them direction.

COMMUNICATION

When you get shot in the head (remember *Regarding Henry*?), the scared one is still there. I don't think that's all that we are, but I think that part of us gets in the way of knowing how to do healthy support—of knowing how to ask for support and to give support when someone makes a mistake.

"I can't believe it Gloria. You mean you don't respect me enough to show up on time? Thank you very much." Somebody does something wrong, and it becomes a reason to reinforce someone else's feelings of inadequacy. And, relative to them, we get to give ourselves a leg up. But sometimes things backfire. Gloria may reply, "I apologize for being late. I had to stop and give somebody CPR on the way up here." Oops.

I want to do my little piece to help create an environment for people to be a little more authentic. In fact, referring to our scared one could be useful. Let's say I've got an issue with someone who intimidates me. Do I want to talk to her about the issue? Does the scared one want to have this conversation? No!

Corrine intimidates me. I've got an issue with her. I do not want to talk to her. Right? I want to talk to Gloria because I feel safe with Gloria. Corrine intimidates me so I'm going to talk to Gloria. So, I come and tell Gloria, "You know I have this issue with Corrine, and I just need some help to deal with it." What can Gloria do to give me healthy support? She could work the triangle option and have the best seat in the house to watch this thing develop. She could intervene and show how adequate she is: "Well, why don't you just let me talk to her for you?"

What I'd like Gloria to say to me is "Well, gee Bowen, it's probably just your scared one being hyperactive, and you're feeling a little inadequate. I don't think you want to allow that to keep you from going in and talking to Corrine about . . ."

I can then go to Corrine and say something like, "You know I appreciate you taking time to visit with me. I have to tell you that I'm a little anxious. You probably don't know this—it's probably not your issue, probably mine—but I'm intimidated by you. But, in spite of the fact that I'm anxious about being here, there is this issue . . . and this is the way I see things. Seeing things this way, this is how I feel. And feeling this way, this is what I need from you in the way of support."

Now, is it likely that she's going to take advantage of my vulnerability? I have no control over that. But why should she? I, in a sense, have already put her one up. I've been real with her, saying what I need in language that's non-threatening.

I'm using "I" messages. I see, I feel, and I need this for me in the way of support. By the way, just because I use "I" messages doesn't mean she's going to give me the healthy support I need. But it increases the likelihood that I will get my needs met if I actually tell someone else what I need. And you know what? Whether or not she does, what I did was heroic.

I go back to Gloria and she says, "Well, how was it Bowen?" I tell her about the conversation. It's never, or rarely, as bad as we think it's going to be. What the scared one inside us does is play out worst-case scenarios to help us avoid risk-taking. If you think you're not creative, look how creative your scared one is when helping you avoid risk-taking. "Oh, shoot, if I go and talk to her, I'll probably mess my shorts." Whatever the situation, the scared one argues that the outcome is going to be something terrible.

FEAR AND NEGATIVITY

This is a core piece of material. I say the driver of the first reel of the movie is fear, and the part of us that has feelings of inadequacy is the scared one. This is a picture of the scared one inside us. The scared one's fearful that at any point we may be exposed as inadequate. The number one fear of people is public speaking. Why? We're vulnerable in an interesting way. [illus.]

110

If we're one-on-one, if I'm just interacting with you, I can tune into you and figure out what kind of performance I have to give to please you. I can try to sense what your needs are and give you that performance. But when I add another person—uh oh. And another and another. How are we supposed to be who everybody needs for us to be to meet their needs? It's a problem, and it comes up when we stand up in front of others. In the spotlight of a group's attention, we run the great risk of being exposed as being inadequate.

The scared one will play out the worst-case scenario. It says that if we reveal ourselves to others, they'll say bad things about us. They'll take advantage of our vulnerability, demote us, won't like us. Our scared one is very creative in a negative way.

I'm a very creative person. Everybody is very creative because everybody has a scared one helping them avoid going anywhere other than where they are and doing anything other than what they already know how to do adequately. But, if we don't allow others to give us our life grade, we can give ourselves an "A" in our book—an "A," not for adequate but for acceptance.

Being scared can be healthy, too. When there's something to be really afraid of, it's healthy to be scared. Fear is a great motivator. I think fear is the driver of the first reel of the movie. It drives our behaviors. In the face of fear, what becomes important is safety and security at all costs, the motto of the scared one.

Fear and negativity are connected. I think it's hard to remain conscious to the alternatives we have when we encounter negative people. It's also exhausting if we expend energy trying to convert them. They are invested in their approach to living.

Some people experience their negativity as a positive. For them it's positive because that's how they experience their power. They have power over others. If we check that out against history, is it true?

Adolf Hitler is an example of someone who was incredibly negative, yet incredibly powerful. He experienced his power by instilling fear in the hearts of others through the use of dominating power, controlling power, power over. Can you think of a reverse case scenario? One in which we see a positive use of power?

Mother Theresa.

Martin Luther King.

Who did Martin Luther King study?

Ghandi.

Who did Mother Theresa study ?

Jesus Christ.

Recognize what happened to Ghandi. What happened to Martin Luther King? What happened to Christ?

They were killed by others through the negative use of power, through power over, because they went against the dominant culture.

But what happened to Hitler? He killed himself.

Is it possible to be successful in the world without exerting power over others? Yes. But the focus isn't on success. It's not on outcome.

There's a wonderful story about a reporter interviewing Mother Theresa. The reporter asks her how it's possible that she could have accomplished so much and been so successful in her work. She replies that she doesn't worry about being successful, just faithful. Remember Victor Frankl, who said,

"Perhaps happiness is like success. It happens precisely because we decide not to think about it"?

When we focus on outcome, the end justifies the means; therefore, we go for efficiency. Whatever it takes to get the result is acceptable.

We get to decide how we're going to be in the world. I think if we talk more about why normal isn't healthy, we'd be able to see when people, including ourselves, are being little Hitlers. We could be clear about what's going on and not give power to the kind of person who seeks to dominate or control others. Ghandi didn't want that kind of power. Christ didn't want that kind of power. Theirs was the power of love and vulnerability.

In an instant, we see how powerful negativity can be. The use of dominating power can get much quicker results than love power. The former uses the dominating form of the Golden Rule. He who has the gold, rules. The latter uses the original version of the Golden Rule: Do unto others as you would have others do unto you.

In our relationships, how can we put into action some of what we are saying? Our initial interaction with others is typically one in which we cooperate, giving others the benefit of the doubt. However, if they are imbalanced and abuse our trust, we can't be naïve. Their behavior is reflective of where they are developmentally, but we don't have to be part of their development. Detach. Pull the plug. Look elsewhere for a partner with whom to collaborate.

We don't have to wait to feel good until that other, imbalanced person is balanced. How can we vaccinate ourselves so that when we're around people like that, we're not allowing them to drive behavior and mood? We can detach with love, detach with compassion. How do we love someone who's not lovable?

113

Think about our energy system. What we often do is take our plug and plug into the socket in other, sometimes imbalanced, people and we allow their juice to drive us. What we've got to do is take the plug and plug it into ourselves and our core values. When we plug it into us, we are moving from an external to an internal point of control. It's also moving from an external reference to an internal reference that's inclusive of our highest values. It's inclusive of the answer to the question, "Why are we here?" Are we simply here to do what the grownups did before? Are we simply here to replicate the status quo? Is that why we're here? I don't think it's enough.

If we think things could be better, how can we make them better? Well, I'll tell you this. I'm a product of the '60s. Guess what? I tried to change the world. Forget it. Don't try to change the world. Don't try to change anybody else. Just work on changing yourself. When I work on changing me, there's always work to do. It's not like, "whoa, I've arrived, you can sit at my feet." When somebody is in that psychological space, they're in a very sick place- the sit at my feet place. I don't think we ever get there. If somebody is there, they wouldn't say so. I'd be highly suspect of hanging out with this person.

But what we're talking about here, this idea of normal not being healthy, is how can we vaccinate ourselves against the negativity, and what can we do in terms of healthy support? Let's say we're in a negative psychological place. Here's a good example of how normal is not healthy: Something unfair happens to you—and your support system says, "The sons of bitches, I can't stand them either. They are to blame. Let's get 'em."

Some people think the way to support you is to help you stay stuck where you are with a friend. They think that's support. But they are really helping us to maintain victim thinking.

Some call that kind of friendship "loyalty." That is loyalty! We honor that. If I'm depressed, how should you be around me? Loyal. If I am depressed, you be depressed. Then we'll be depressed together. It's the loyalty of the child.

How does it feel being around depressed people? Depressing. That reaction is the cultural norm. If somebody is depressed, it's disrespectful to be chipper, to be up if they are down.

And so we're afraid to be honest.

One thing I've discovered is that it doesn't help me to be depressed with my depressed patients. Somebody comes in and I say, "How's it going today?" "It's the worst, it's just terrible. It's the worst, worst, terrible, terrible thing."

"Have you thought of killing yourself? I think, as bad as that sounds, you might want to consider ending it all. I don't know if you want to go on living, as bad as that sounds."

Does it help for me to be depressed with my depressed patient? No, but that's what we tend to do. When I'm playing the role of the victim, I want someone to give me healthy support. I don't want someone to help me stay stuck where I am with a friend.

Everybody's at a different stage in their own personal evolution. Guess what I can do in a millisecond? In a heartbeat I can revert back to all the old, still familiar patterns. There's all that residual material in my psyche: poor me senarios. I don't like that, I don't want to do that, but I still do it. But, I have people I can call on the phone, people with whom I can hang out, to mirror back to me when I am in that victim mentality.

In Twelve Step programs there are sponsors to provide individual support. But normal people, what have we got? Normal people have a lot of folks who stay stuck with them. And it's an unempowered role. In fact it's worth picking a daisy here connected to this whole victim consciousness as norm.

THE VICTIM

The Human Service Alliance (HAS) is a community of people in North Carolina who share a common interest in service. They have different service projects for people of need in their community. Volunteers apply to be able to serve with the HAS. And if they're accepted, they go through a training program that helps clear the air around many personal issues, including the issue of victim thinking.

The following is an excerpt on playing the victim from *Better Than Money Can Buy*, an HAS publication that talks about their work in North Carolina.

[Pgs 75-78 Better Than Money Can Buy]

A Generalized "Victim Statement"

The essence of victim mentality is represented by the following statement:

If things are going wrong, or badly, or not to my liking , then someone is to blame. It is necessary to identify the person(s), circumstance(s), or source(s) of why things are not as I think they should be. Blame must be determined, and it must be accepted by the wrongdoer. I must be vindicated. My emotional upset is justified. The bad things that happen to me are not opportunities for learning or growth.

Statements Which Indicate Victim Mentality

Look what you made me do.

You hurt my feelings.

It's your/his/her/their/God's fault.

Can you believe what she did to me?

If you'd straighten up your act, we could get along.

I didn't do a thing to her and look what she did to me.

I'm sick and tired of...

When you do that, it just drives me nuts.

I can't help it, that's just the way I am.

If only he wouldn't/weren't/didn't...

Nothing I do makes any difference.

If you really loved me, you would/wouldn't...

It's all her fault.

I'm always so busy doing for everybody else, I never have time for myself.

I'm that way because of my terrible childhood.

I don't love myself enough yet, and until I do...

There you go again; you keep doing that to me.

We always have to do what *you* want to do.

I've told you a thousand times that I don't like that.

He just doesn't care about me or he would not do that.

I do all the giving around here and get nothing in return.

I've been abused by people all my life.

My boss doesn't appreciate me.

My kids don't appreciate all I do for them.

It's because of you that I have this headache.

You just don't know the misery you have caused me.

If it weren't for me, you'd be a nobody.

You've hurt me for the last time.

Why does this always happen to me?

Why me?

You make me so mad/frustrated/angry, etc.

Everything happens to me.

If it weren't for those children of his, I could be nicer.

She made me do this. I didn't want to, but...

He is always looking out for himself. What about me?

People just don't care anymore. The will take advantage of you every chance they get.

I'm so busy, I just don't have time to do anything I like.

He *made* me...

Life is really difficult for me.

If you can't do your part, I'm certainly not going to do mine!

Do you really love me?

If you're willing to help, that's great. If not, I'll struggle through by myself.

They messed me all up.

They need to be taught a lesson.

I want to make sure they won't ever do this to someone else.

You can't fight the system.

You don't know how I have suffered.

I've suffered more (so I deserve more).

Life is like that. That's life.

If it's not one thing, it's another.

A woman's work is never done.

You can't win for losing.

I only want what's fair.

It wasn't *my* idea (i.e. you can't blame me).

You just don't understand.

If only you had...

It's too late now (the damage is done).

Hey, look! I'm the victim in all this!

They just won't listen to me (or do what I say, etc.).

You'll be sorry.

I won't forget this.

Nobody understands me.

Boy, are they gonna miss me when I'm gone.

Nobody loves me.

My life will never be the same.

Ain't it awful?

If you'd been through what I've been through...

They done me wrong.

After all I did for them, this is what I get.

What did I do to deserve this?

I never thought they'd treat me this way.

My job is driving me crazy.

I'm not responsible for what happened.

My spouse/child/relative/friend/boss/paperboy/hairdresser is driving me crazy.

You have no idea what I do all day.

Nobody else works as hard as I do.

Ugh! I can't eat that. It looks awful.

My parents are driving me crazy.

My parents don't understand me.

The doctors made a mess of me.

If only the government weren't so bad.

I am surrounded by idiots.

People are so insensitive.

I am not getting what I deserve.

My husband is so insensitive.

The schools are ruining my children.

My in-laws are ruining my children.

Some people have all the luck.

Why do you keep doing this to me?

Why do you always pick on me?

My ex-spouse is ruining my children.

You mean I am supposed to do that all by myself?

You can't trust anyone over 30.

You can't trust anyone under 30.

Someone has got to suffer for what happened to me!

There is no way out of this mess.

They showed me no respect-treated me like dirt!

I always got the worst teachers and the worst bosses.

Anyone in my situation would be as angry as I am!

I'm not responsible for how I react.

Let's get away from being victims and talk about giving healthy support. As a physician, when people come to see me, they honor me. They allow me to participate in their lives in a meaningful way. Guess what happens when I allow other people to support me? I do the same thing. I honor them. And guess what I've discovered? People like it. They like participating in my life in a meaningful way. I like it too. It is such a relief. I'm accepted as I am. I can be vulnerable. They won't go away. There's no "if" clause in the relationship. They care. I feel their caring. It doesn't mean they tell me what I want to hear, but they do tell me what I need to hear. It's so great to have that healthy support. A lot of people who are normal, but not healthy, don't have that kind of support.

RUMI

How would you like another Rumi poem? It's connected to this whole idea of support.

"If you are separated from those in spiritual labor

You are thrown down. You are a part without its whole. And if the enemy of ecstasy finds anyone cut off from that whole, he experiences him all alone and eats him up."

Coleman Barks, the person who best translates Rumi, has a calling. We're all supposed to figure out what the heck our calling is. Coleman Barks was a professor at the University of Georgia in Athens and just recently retired. He had never heard of Rumi until 1976, when Robert Bly gave him a book and told him, "These poems need to be released from their cages." Barks started working on Rumi translations then and has been doing it every morning since.

When Barks was growing up, he lived in the Tennessee Valley. His dad was the headmaster of a school. When Barks was only five or six years old, he got a hold of the 1943 *Rand McNally Atlas* and memorized all the capitals of every country in the world.

Barks took meals with four hundred kids and teachers daily. One of the things that his dining room mates did at meals was to shout out a country, and Coleman would shout out the capital.

One day he was eating, and this Latin teacher yelled out, "Capadocia." He went through his mind and didn't know what it was. He couldn't answer the question and, from that moment on, he was known at the school as "Cappy," or "Cap."

Much later in his life, after he'd begun to translate Rumi's poems into American free verse, Barks was looking at an ancient map. Barks, who knew that Rumi had spent most of his life in Konya, Turkey, noticed that the capital of Capadocia was . . . Konya. That got his attention.

The Capadocia event happened when Barks was five or six-years-old. Forty years later, after he was well into his Rumi work, he made this connection. He made other connections and you can read about some of them in *The Glance: Songs of Soul-Meeting*, a book of Rumi translations.

An important connection for Rumi was a special friend and mentor named Shams, a mystic wanderer from Tabriz. When Shams and Rumi met they had this very powerful spiritual connection and would spend lengthy periods of time talking with each other in spiritual reverie. Shams was Rumi's healthy support system.

This relationship made Rumi's students jealous because when Shams was around, Rumi wanted to spend time with him instead of with the students. Shams was mysteriously killed one day, and nobody knows exactly what happened. A lot of people think he was murdered by Rumi's students.

All of Rumi's poetry came out of his friendship with Shams. Before that relationship, Rumi had been a scholar who hadn't composed any of his own work. But after meeting Shams, Rumi spontaneously erupted poems that joyously leap through seven hundred and fifty years to enlighten us today. He understood paradox.

He has a short little poem that says:
"How can this great love be inside me?
I'm so small, I can barely be seen.
Well, the eye is small yet it holds enormous things."

Go out at night, when the sky is clear, see what the eye beholds. How could this great love be inside me, when I feel so inadequate! That's the paradox.

Shams had been swimming on the other side of the metaphorical aquarium looking for a spiritual companion. He found Rumi. Once Sham's was killed, Rumi had already gone over into the new. He had begun to swim into mystical reality that he, as a scholar, had read about his whole life. With Shams' encouragement, Rumi left dry land for that wetness and became green and juicy, dripping with nourishment for his community. His poetry was his gift, his work/play in the world. He couldn't have done it alone. Neither can we.

Sometimes we don't feel up to the work, up to the play, up to the task, up to all that we are called upon to do. But, what if we don't have to do it alone? What if we get help? My bias is, if you ask, you get help. But, be selective whom you ask.

CHAPTER 10

BEING PLASTIC

I thought what we might do is start out this section with a little quote from Ashley Montagu, from his book *Growing Young*, on the evolution of human behavior. The wonderful thing about Montagu is that he's both a very good writer and has all this scientific data to support his ideas. Remember that neoteny is the whole idea that we are meant to retain the wonderful traits of the child thoughout development. "It is by the neoteony of plasticity, of malleability, of adaptability that the made-over ape became *Homo sapiens*, and it is upon the continued development of these same neontenous traits that his further evolution depends."

He then quotes William Kingdon Clifford, who in the late 1800s said that "the first condition of mental development is that the mind should be creative rather than acquisitive."

Sounds like Einstein: "Imagination is more important than knowledge."

Clifford goes on to say that "if we consider that a race, in proportion as it is plastic and capable of change, may be regarded as young and vigorous, while a race which is fixed, persistent in form, unable to change, is as surely effete, worn out, in peril of extinction; we shall see, I think, the immense importance to a nation of checking the growth of conventionalities. It is quite possible for conventional rules of action and conventional habits of thought to get such

Personally, I think it's difficult to change without the participation of some power greater than ourselves. What I do when I'm fearful, resonating at the scared one's frequency, is to sit on a lap of some omniscient, omnipotent, and omnipresent mystery that is beyond my understanding, that I can not possibly fathom. In that lap I'm loved and accepted as I am, flaws and all. There's no "if" clause. It's not "if" I do something in the way of improvement then I'm going to be an accepted member of the family. I'm loved and accepted just as I am.

If the motto of my scared guy is safety and security at all costs, how can I really feel safe and secure? Through material things? No. I take my scared one, sit on that lap, feel loved and accepted, and accept my inheritance. We get inheritance from the culture. But I think we have another inheritance. I think there's another family system and in it, you're all my brothers and sisters. In that family system I'm loved and accepted by my Higher Power: Father, Mother, God. Feeling the grace of that love is a safety net. I feel safe.

Feeling safe and secure, I can risk more exposure on the world's stage.

I can go back to my old ways and forget about the safety net. When I'm feeling insecure and inadequate, what can I do to experience self-acceptance, flaws and all? I can use my highest values to support me, to hold me up, safely.

I wish I did more lap sitting. After all, what are our values for?

But I also have friends, other nuts, to help me to remember. I think it's hard, but it's sort of like stress management. It's as far away as your next thought. What am I going for? Perfect? Okay, I screwed up. I didn't do it right. I could have done it better. I could have given a better presentation. I could have been more articulate. I could have been more compassionate.

Personally, I think it's difficult to change without the participation of some power greater than ourselves. What I do when I'm fearful, resonating at the scared one's frequency, is to sit on a lap of some omniscient, omnipotent, and omnipresent mystery that is beyond my understanding, that I can not possibly fathom. In that lap I'm loved and accepted as I am, flaws and all. There's no "if" clause. It's not "if" I do something in the way of improvement then I'm going to be an accepted member of the family. I'm loved and accepted just as I am.

If the motto of my scared guy is safety and security at all costs, how can I really feel safe and secure? Through material things? No. I take my scared one, sit on that lap, feel loved and accepted, and accept my inheritance. We get inheritance from the culture. But I think we have another inheritance. I think there's another family system and in it, you're all my brothers and sisters. In that family system I'm loved and accepted by my Higher Power: Father, Mother, God. Feeling the grace of that love is a safety net. I feel safe.

Feeling safe and secure, I can risk more exposure on the world's stage.

I can go back to my old ways and forget about the safety net. When I'm feeling insecure and inadequate, what can I do to experience self-acceptance, flaws and all? I can use my highest values to support me, to hold me up, safely.

I wish I did more lap sitting. After all, what are our values for?

But I also have friends, other nuts, to help me to remember. I think it's hard, but it's sort of like stress management. It's as far away as your next thought. What am Igoing for? Perfect? Okay, I screwed up. I didn't do it right. I could have done it better. I could have given a better presentation. I could have been more articulate. I could have been more compassionate.

My feelings can also be a reminder. Where are they coming from? What can I learn from them? Well I learned that I could be the thoughtless in certain circumstances that make me feel vulnerable. I can watch myself, and in watching I can find the energy to do something different because I'm paying attention.

So if I accept that I can be dishonest, for instance, I can watch how I communicate. And when I'm right there on the edge of a lie, I can re-decide, say something honest, risk more, and be more vulnerable because, often, dishonesty is about self-protection.

In terms of just the honesty piece, here's an example of normal not being healthy. Have you ever been to some kind of communication seminar? What did you hear the biggest problem with communication was? Listening. We do not listen. People talk. We do not listen. Right. And how many ears do we have? Three: two on our head and one in the chest. It's heart, h-ear-t.

I think listening is very important and I agree that it's an issue, but it's not the biggest problem we have with communication. If you're listening to me and I'm lying to you, are we really making contact?

The biggest problem we have is we don't risk being honest. When we were growing up we heard that honesty was the best policy. But what happened when we were honest? We got in trouble. So what did we learn to do? Lie. Survival at all costs, right?

In 1959 Tom Powers wrote a book called *First Question in the Life of the Spirit*. He did a spiritual quest and wrote this wonderful book, which came out more recently under another title, *Invitation to a Great Experiment*.

Powers joined Alcoholics Anonymous (AA) in its early years, in 1942. In the book he talks about the idea of AAA: All Addicts Anonymous, because his belief is that everybody's addicted to something. Everybody, at one point or another, allows the scared one to turn to some unhealthy person, place, or thing/ behavior or substance to numb their feelings of inadequacy.

In 1985, a group of us lead by a man named Don Campbell, got together and did this small group process with the book. We would get together for ninety minutes a week and talk about how to have the experience of God in our lives. We used the book, reading three or four pages every week. We paraphrased what we read to better understand it, then met to discuss what we'd read. We got to about page ninety and recognized that we hadn't been doing what the book was talking about, and we went back and started over. It's not easy getting healthy.

One of the things Tom Powers talks about is honesty, and when I came to this piece in the book I thought, okay, next issue. If there was one thing I was, it was honest. I don't even like being around dishonest people.

Now, as a kid growing up, in my family system, I got in trouble a lot. If I had been honest with my parents it would have been counter to survival. When I was in college, my parents heard I was experimenting with drugs and confronted me about it. I was twenty-three years old and for the first time in my adult life I'd decided to be completely honest with them. To finally be able to tell them the truth about everything I was into was a great relief to me.

It felt so good I decided that from that point onward in my life I was going to be honest. I used to be dishonest but not any more. At least, that's what I believed.

Before my wife and I got married, we cohabitated briefly. I was an honest person and told my mom about it. But, I didn't tell her parents. Why didn't I tell her parents?

Was I really being honest, or was I being selectively honest? I was selectively honest. I think my degree of honesty also had something to do with the fact that her father had played goalie on the University of Wisconsin's hockey team and center on its football team. I think that might have had something to do with it. And he didn't like guys with ponytails. See how we can rationalize? It's so easy to do.

What the Tom Powers' book made me do is confront my own dishonesty. By accepting that I could at times be dishonest, I could begin to work on becoming honest. As long as I don't accept that I can be dishonest, then I'm going to continue to deceive people with or without awareness. You can deceive people without even lying. Silence is a way to deceive.

I actually recognize that I have made progress in this area. I risk a lot more than I used to. But guess what? I can still be dishonest, without ever telling a lie. I want to keep an eye on how I communicate. I want to keep watching. I want to keep paying attention to what I'm doing with some awareness. So, I have to take the flashlight of my attention and shine it on my efforts to communicate honestly.

THE OBSERVER "I"

Like two golden birds perched on the selfsame tree, intimate friends, the ego and the self dwell in the same body. The former eats the sweet and sour fruits of life, while the latter looks on in detachment.

--The Mundaka Upanishad

130

What would happen if we could look down upon ourselves—observe our behavior and our life—from a higher or greater perspective? The idea of watching ourselves—paying attention to what we do and to how we feel doing it--is central to being healthy. We have to be watching what we're doing because that's the only way we can take action with awareness.

And here's the kicker: Just by watching—our behavior changes. We don't have to be self-critical. We don't have to be demeaning. We don't have to be judgmental. All we have to do is watch. So when I'm talking to someone else, if I'm paying attention, watching, I can change. I can risk being more open and honest. It's the observer effect.

Here's an example we can probably all relate to—holiday cooking. You're a kid, and you smell cookies baking in the kitchen. These are holiday cookies, and what do kids like? Cookies! You want some, and your olfactory apparatus has engaged your limbic system to signal the cortex to move your body toward the kitchen. And you go in and the baker is there and says, "You don't want to spoil your appetite."

But you are given a little bit of dough, a cookie, or whatever it happens to be. Is that enough? Is it enough? No. It is not enough. So you say, "Come on, I want some more. I'll finish my supper. I promise...pleeeease."

You get stonewalled. But, you're not undone. You play like you're leaving, but you keep your fingers on the pulse of the activity in the kitchen. And when the grownup leaves the kitchen, what do you do? You go in there and nail some more. And you're just reaching up, grabbing, when the baker walks in.

Nothing has to be said. Just because you're being watched, your behavior changes.

All we have to do is watch. All we have to do is pay attention, and our behavior changes. It's the observer effect.

G. I. Gurdjieff was an enigmatic teacher who came to Europe in 1915. It is said that he traveled around Asia for twenty-five years by himself, studying with different people.

He starts a school in France and teaches his students about the concept of watching, among other things, as a first step in becoming fully human. He talks about the observer "I" and the personality "I." Each of us has an observer "I." And the observer "I" needs to be paying attention to what the personality "I" is doing. And when the observer "I" pays attention to what the personality is doing, what the personality does is different.

It's the idea presented above in the story about the two birds. And that's something we can all do. But guess what? Because normal isn't healthy, few do. Part of being normal is to see ourselves as one entity, namely, the personality. That second one, the observer, is present but not able to be helpful until recognized and valued.

Even then, we fall asleep, back into the cultural trance. I'm watching myself, I'm watching . . . I fall asleep; I have psychological narcolepsy. Even though I'm wide awake, I'm asleep. In a nanosecond I can forget everything I know—I'm asleep. Automatic pilot. Cruise Control. It's like, "Well what the hell happened?" And do you know what I need? I need other people in my life. I need other people to watch me, too, when I doze off, because I do doze off.

I can watch what I do, but I can also pay attention to what I'm not doing. It's not that I care about how productive I have been or how productive I am. Relative to what I'm capable of doing, I'm scratching the surface. I know that.

For example, I've been writing this book for more than ten years. Have you ever heard of the term sloth? Do you know that moss sometimes actually grows on a sloth--that sloths have moss? This is a fact. I'm beginning to inspect myself for moss. I'm watching for moss.

I started writing this book in 1989. Why did it take me so long to finish the project? Why? I'll tell you why.

Not finishing means not risking. If I finish the book, someone might actually read it. I risk others rejecting my ideas. And I would that rejection, that potential criticism, personally. Having my feelings of inadequacy reinforced feels so bad that I sabotage completion. I kill the book and slay those feelings before they occur *in reality.*

My scared one plays out worst-case scenarios to avoid exposure to rejection. I stay safe by not finishing the book. Then no one can read it to find out how stupid, unoriginal, banal, and superfluous I am.

Those thoughts are a perfect example of why normal isn't healthy. My scared one will avoid risk-taking and, therefore, the anxiety inherent with the risk. Risk management to the scared one means to avoid being seen as a flop or a failure in the eyes of the world. By not finishing the book, or certain other projects, for that matter, I decrease my exposure. Playing out the rejection in my imagination reinforces my feelings of inadequacy.

As a risk manager, my scared one downsizes risk by presenting reason after reason to put off completion: *Why should anyone read this book? There are so* many good books out there already. *What makes me think I have anything to add? It will be so hard to organize my material in a concise way for the reader. Besides it will take away from other fun stuff that I really enjoy.*

And when sitting down to write, to work through the internal resistance the scared one creates, distraction is always one thought away:

You know, I think I'll get something to eat.

Look at that floor. I can't believe It's so dirty. If the floor were clean, I could write better.

I need some exercise. Yeah, that's the ticket. I'll write better, concentrate better, after I work out and shower.

The irony of it is that the scared one is endlessly creative in the distractions he presents to keep me from the task. He will map out detour after detour to avoid reaching the end.

And then, to add insult to injury, he says: *You really are pathetic! You'll never finish that book. You've been blowing smoke for years. Why don't you just forget it!*

I keep seeing the same issues coming up over and over and over, but I see that developmentally I'm making some progress. But I have to keep relearning how I make progress. I have to keep remembering and being reminded of my neotenous traits: adaptability, plasticity, malleability, and experimental mindedness.

Remembering this might be useful to you. You might think of some premature cognitive commitments that you've made, revisit them, and say, "Maybe I do want to take another risk. I'd risked that before and didn't want to fail again, but I am, afterall, neotenous."

You may fall on your face, but just knowing that provides a little cushion for the psyche. And don't forget Rumi's poem about falling and finding your wings. ("They fall and in falling they're given wings.") When we fall, we have to remember we're really growing flight feathers. And when our friends, our significant other, or our children fall, perhaps there is a feather or two popping out.

"The way of love is not a subtle argument. The door there is devastation." Had a relationship that didn't work? Great. What did you learn? If we want to do a little flying, we're going to fall. It hurts. We just need to give ourselves permission to fall enough until we learn what it is we need to learn to have relationships that are healthy.

I asked a group of people once, "What do you say to yourselves when you make a mistake? Just about everyone said self-deprecating things. But one woman raised her hand and said that when she makes a mistake she says, "Oh."

I said, "When you make a mistake you say to yourself, 'oh?'" She said, "That's right."

I said, "Stand in a corner and straighten yourself out. That's suspiciously healthy, I'm giving your name to the thought police." And then I said, "Why do you say oh?" And she said, "O-H, only *h*uman."

I said, "Did you always say that?" She said, "Oh no. I used to be an incredible perfectionist and then had years of therapy."

Folks, save yourselves some money! We can change. One thing that separates us from other animals is our ability to change. We possess the neotenous traits of the child--daptability, flexibility, plasticity, experimental mindedness. All of these traits are connected to this process of being able to change.

Montagu said it best. "Plasticity is beyond all other traits the most neotenous. . . . The outstanding capacity of humankind is its educibility. . . . Natural selection on the human level favors gene complexes which enable their possessors to adjust their behavior to any condition in the light of previous experience."

So we can learn. What else can we do to be healthy, to have healthier relationships with other people, to be more effective at what we do, and to have more fun getting better? All of that requires learning, and in the process of learning something new, we're going to make mistakes.

The problem is that when we make mistakes, we feel inadequate. I think the "O-H" woman had a good idea. In fact I think we ought to interchange the way we deal with mistake making and sneezing. Somebody sneezes and what do we say? "God bless you." Somebody makes a mistake, what do we say? "You dumb shit!" I think we should just switch them. If somebody makes a mistake we say, "God bless you. You're only human." Somebody sneezes we say, "You dumb shit. Why are blowing germs all over the room?" Mistakes are much more frequent than sneezes. We'd be doing much more blessing than cursing.

Who benefits if we love and accept ourselves with our flaws? Everybody. Why does everybody benefit? The more loving and accepting I am of myself with my flaws, the more loving and accepting I am when flaws show up in other people. Because the way I treat other people, isn't about how I feel about them; it's about how I feel about me. What happens when we're having a little trouble with that? What then?

Juggling is a wonderful metaphor for learning. Have you ever picked up some balls or fruit and tried to juggle? Did you learn?

Juggling is something that almost everybody has tried. You try juggling, something that you've never tried before, and you fail. So you have a good reason for why you can't juggle. I mean, if you've tried it, you learned it's not easy. Balls keep dropping. It takes practice. Did you think, "Well, I'm just not that coordinated"? Or, you see somebody else try it, and she picks it up pretty quickly?

We compare ourselves with other people. We see how quickly they learn something, compare ourselves with them, and feel inadequate. And we say, "Well, I've tried it and I couldn't do it." And we say, "I can't do it. I mean it's not my fault. I tried. I just can't do it." Do your kids ever tell you that? "I can't find it! It's not in here. I looked." And you go into the room and in thirty seconds you find it.

"I can't" means *it's not my fault*. "It's not my fault" is another way of getting into the victim mindset. We tend not to use the contraction *won't* because it connotes ownership. "Well, I'm just not willing to do that. It's not that I can't. I just won't."

My bias is that everyone can learn to juggle, but few people do learn. I haven't met anybody who can't learn to juggle. The trouble is, you try something new, you don't get it right away, and you think," *I can't*. I'm not a natural if I don't get it right away." I'd like you to consider that that may be a premature cognitive commitment.

Earlier we talked about how we learn to see self and world and about how that learning creates limits on our ability to fully function and unfold our potential as people. We make premature cognitive commitments. We learn how to think about self and world and that creates limits, or conceptual boundaries.

Now, someone says, "Can you juggle?" You say, "No, I can't do it. Been there done that." You tap into your database of life experience, where you've stored the memory and the belief that you've tried but can't do it. Wait . . . Is it can't or won't? Are you willing to fail enough to earn the right to be successful?

I learned to juggle in medical school. There's a secret to juggling. The secret to juggling is . . .? You don't earn the right to have the skill until you fail enough to get it. What happens when you drop the balls enough? You quit dropping them. When you've dropped them enough you now know how to juggle.

So you earn the right to have the skill by failing enough to get it. How many times do you have to drop the balls? Just enough. The learning curve is going to be different for every person. Juggling requires a unique set of skills, and some people acquire these skills more quickly than others do, but almost everybody can juggle. So don't worry about it. "Enough" will occur when you no longer drop the balls.

You can make it easier on yourself. You can throw the balls while standing in front of a wall so they don't go out of the plane parallel to your body. You can practice over a bed so you don't have to keep bending over so far, and so they don't roll so far away. But you're going to have to drop them. When you've dropped them over, and over, and over, and dropped them enough, you've earned the right to know how to juggle.

The problem is that when we try something new and fail, we use our failure as a reason to reinforce our feelings of inadequacy. "I can't juggle. I'm not coordinated. I can't learn that. I've tried that before and I've never been good at sports."

We have a relationship that doesn't work out. We think, *been there, done that.* If we choose to not try it again, guess what? It's not that we can't have a good relationship with somebody out there. It means that we're not willing to risk failrue again because it hurt so bad.

So, what if we change the charge on making mistakes? What if we change the charge on failing so it doesn't have a negative connotation? What if we give ourselves permission to fail in the process of learning how to do new stuff?

There are risks involved. How can we create a support system so that when we make mistakes, people will help us get through them? In your work groups, do you have mistake-of-the-month meetings, where people get together, step forward, and share their best mistakes? Why don't we do that in family systems or organizational systems? Because in our culture, there's only one way of doing things and that's the right way.

We honor our victories and successes but have trouble with our defeats, losses, and failures. And it's sad because defeats, losses, and failures are what we have to go through to learn how to be more fully us, to be more fully able to express our gifts. We're going to have to go through the mistake-making process.

At Christmas, a few years after I learned to juggle, my wife got me juggling pins. I opened up the present and thought, *Oh boy, new toy.* I got out the pins, with all four girls around the tree, and the spotlight was on me. Guess what? I couldn't juggle the pins. Guess how I felt failing in front of my children? I was feeling a little inadequate and so decided to practice in private, where nobody could see me fail. I'd disappear and, like magic, come back with the skill so everyone could see how adequate I am.

So, I went limping off to practice in private—and then I had this *ah ha!* Wait a second! I don't want to fail in private. I want to fail in public. I want my kids to see me fail over and over, get frustrated, and not quit. So that's what I did. I failed over and over and over, and after I dropped the pins enough I finally learned how to juggle them.

What happened was simple. I remembered my own belief system: B.L.E.F. Anything I do I can do *Better* if I'm willing to *Learn*. But I *Earn* my learning the old fashion way by *Failing* enough to get it. I think that's a key piece to learning. If we're going to break out of old patterns and generate new, healthier responses to stressful life events, there's going to be a learning curve to grow through.

Sometimes we're lucky, and we get it on the first try. But most of the time that isn't the case. We may get frustrated but that's just because we haven't practiced enough and failed enough. It doesn't matter what it is that we're learning. It's trial and error. That's the way science works. That's the way we learned as kids. We were little scientists. The experimental-minded child is doing science all the time, doing trials and making errors. That neoteny needs to continue throughout the life cycle, not just in childhood.

Part of normal not being healthy is what happens to development. There's all this incredible development from zero to seven, from birth to the age of reason. It's amazing what happens. To watch the whole thing unfold is absolutely awe-inspiring. Seven is the age of reason.

Then, from seven to fourteen, from the age of reason to puberty, there is also a lot of development. From fourteen to twenty-one, puberty to late adolescence/early adulthood, quite a bit of development takes place. And then you have a little less from twenty-one to twenty-eight; twenty-eight to thirty-five; thirty-five to forty-two; forty-two to forty-nine; forty-nine to fifty-six; fifty-six to sixty-three. What happens to development? It slows way down.

In fact, our own personal evolution may stop long before our movie is over. We slip into a box, long before a coffin, and dry up long before we're dust.

We learn how to do our important grownup stuff. We learn how to do our job. We learn how to handle responsibilities, and we establish that we're adequate. We learn to do things in an adequate fashion, and the tendency is to keep doing what we know how to do. We establish that we're adequate or competent at something, and the scared one inside feels comfortable repeating those task-specific behaviors.

But in terms of going into the new or exploring areas that we might have explored in the past and experienced pain, disappointment or failure, the tendency is to think, *been there, done that.* Is it possible that we made premature cognitive commitments? Maybe we can do it. Maybe we just haven't been willing to enter back into that sometimes painful and frustrating learning process.

Remember what the evolutionary intelligence has shown us. Our most neotenous human trait is "plasticity" and we are "educibile," throughout the life cycle.

REVIEW OF THE FIRST REEL OF THE MOVIE

Let's review the implications of the dynamic of the first reel of the movie. What's the driver of the first reel of the movie? Fear. What's the driver of the stress response? Fear is the driver of the stress response, and the stress response is a survival response.

In the face of fear what is important is survival, and we can survive our whole lives but never live them. Survival is not the same as thriving. Survival is a beginning.

In the first reel of the movie of our lives what are the implications for our relationships? We are dependent initially and then codependent. *We have these feelings of inadequacy but we don't want anyone to know.*

What's the other side the coin of codependency? What's the other side of the coin of normal not being healthy? As a child we learn to be compliant or defiant. In both of these the focus is on the external reference. We can be compliant with our peers while we are defiant to authority figures. But in both of these positions, we're neglectful of our own interior.

We learn to be neglectful of our own needs but, guess what? We also learn to be self centered. In the first reel of the movie we are egocentric yet don't know how to act in our own best self-interest. We concern ourselves with our image in the eyes of other people. The scared one doesn't want people to know its secret feelings of inadequacy, so we project an image we think others want to see.

Why do we neglect our needs and focus on meeting the needs of other people? So we can get our needs met on the return. Because we're codependent, we're externally referented; we're focusing "out there" and looking for the "fix" to come from the environment. We learn that the emptiness inside is filled from the outside in. We move from empty to full by virtue of consumption.

We have a medical establishment that participates, providing the "fix" for the community to keep it off bottom. We're trained to be a physician. The word *physician* is derived from a word that means "medicine, or medication." We're taught in medical school to be physicians rather than doctors. *Doctor* is derived from a word that means "teacher." So we're medicators instead of educators. (Maria Montessori broke the mold.) The problem is, sometimes it works.

We're able, as physicians, to provide the "fix." You're depressed, here take one of these; you're anxious, here take one of these. You're bipolar, here take one of these. Whatever it is you have is the result of a biochemical imbalance in your brain, and if you take this pill, it will balance you out. It's not your fault you have a biochemical imbalance in your brain. All of this works with the system, with your training, because you're dependent upon the doctor, the external referent, to give you the "fix," the consumption, for the problem.

There's no learning involved other than the fact that you now know you've got a screwed up biochemical thing in your brain and you need a pill to compensate for that chemical thing with which you were born. There's no reason to do any talking or changing because it's the biochemical imbalance that we need to correct. Physical ailments get much the same physician response. "You have high blood pressure, here's a pill. You chose the wrong parents . . . . And so it goes.

Learning about the body-mind connection allows us to learn how to do what some pills do. The fix isn't in a pill; it's within our own being. But we're usually not doing that in the first reel of the movie. In the first reel of the movie

143

the dynamic with which we're functioning is normal and externally focused. We're passive and dependent upon authority figures, doctors, to supply the "fix" for our problems. In medicine, we call it managed care and we talk about medical management. This is another example of why normal isn't healthy.

I was watching CNN one time and they had a management consultant taking calls from around the country. Somebody called up and said, "How do you manage your boss?" "Well, you manage up the same way as you manage down. There are three basic rules of management: observe, predict, control. First you observe the person you want to control. Then, after you've observed them, you can then predict what they're going to do. Once you can predict what they're going to do, you can then control them. Observe. Predict. Control. So what's another implication here in the first reel of the movie? Manipulation.

We are discussing the *implications of the first reel of the movie of our normal, but not necessarily healthy, life.* We're born dependent. We're taught to be codependent. We survive our lives driven by fear. We all have feelings of inadequacy and insecurity that we don't want other people to know about. We project images of adequacy and security to others that compensate for those feelings of inadequacy, so no one knows our secret.

Perhaps, if we could talk about this secret we could address relationship problems from another perspective, one inclusive of our own baggage. Then, our differences would be less of a barrier because our secret would be a bridge that connects us together.

That would, however, require openness and honesty. And that is not something we risk too frequently in the first reel. Junior comes home from school and goes in the kitchen to get something to eat. He takes his food out into the TV room and sees his dad sitting, bent over, in a chair with his head is in his hands, shaking his head.

The son can see that something is troubling his father. So, he says, "Gee, dad, what's wrong?" Quickly, what do you think dad says?

"Nothing." Exactly.

Why does dad say "nothing?" Besides the fact that dad's dad probably said the same thing when asked, we can think of plenty of reasons. He didn't want to worry his son. His son would not have been able to understand. His son couldn't do anything to help. It was too complicated to go into. Or, because of this secret we've been discussing, he may not have wanted to be vulnerable, to reveal his scary feelings and be seen as inadequate.

So, what does he do? He, for all the right reasons, lies to his teenage son. And, what does the son learn from this exchange? He has just been handed the baton from his father. Now, if he has a problem that may worry or upset his dad, or that his father couldn't understand, or that his dad couldn't do anything about, he knows what to say.

"How's it goin', son?"

"Fine."

"Any problems?"

"Nope."

Why should our children be vulnerable with us when it's follow the leader? All parents are leaders. Our example, as parents, speaks volumes. What we don't say is heard clearly.

THE SECOND *REAL* OF THE MOVIE

CHAPTER 11

LOVE'S CONFUSING JOY

Rumi has another poem I'd like to share with you.

Love is taken away my practices and filled me with poetry,

I tried to keep quietly repeating, 'No strength but yours,' but I couldn't,

I had to clap and sing,

I used to be respectable, and chased, and stable,

But who can stand in this strong wind, and remember those things,

A mountain keeps an echo deep inside itself, that's how I hold your voice,

I am scrap wood thrown in your fire and quickly reduced to smoke,

I saw you a became empty

This emptiness, more beautiful than existence, it obliterates existence,

And yet when it comes, existence thrives and creates more existence,

The sky is blue

The world is a blind man squatting on the road

But whoever sees your emptiness sees beyond blue and beyond the blind man,

A great soul hides like Mohammed, or Jesus, moving through a crowd in a city where no one knows him

To praise is to praise how one surrenders to the emptiness

To praise the sun is to praise your own eyes

Praise the ocean, what we say a little ship

So the sea journey goes on and who knows where

Just to be held by the ocean is the best luck we could have

It's a total waking up

Why should we grieve that we've been sleeping

It doesn't matter how long we've been unconscious

We're groggy, but let the guilt go

Feel the motions of tenderness around you, the buoyancy

Feel the motions of tenderness around you. The buoyancy. Doesn't matter how long we've been sleeping. Let the guilt go.

When we're feeling the emptiness, we do not honor it. We choose instead to look to the outside for something to come into us. My friend Don Campbell describes the emptiness as a "God-shaped vacuum." We can try to fill that vacuum with our addictive behaviors that medicate our discomfort and with our multitasking behaviors to prove our worth, but that will never be enough. But if we allow ourselves to just be with the emptiness, we experience the truth of the paradox "less is more. "

In the first reel of the movie, we have trouble with the emptiness. We don't like the feeling. It's uncomfortable. We look for something tangible to get our hands on or some affirmation from the cosmos for comfort. In the second real of the movie—notice the different spelling—we open to that discomfort and experience it as longing. The dynamic of the first reel of the movie is outside in. What's the driver of the first reel of the movie? Fear. The driver of the second real of the movie is love.

Rumi has another short poem: "If you want what visible reality can give, you're an employee. If you want the unseen world, you're not living your truth.

Both wishes are foolish. But you'll be forgiven for forgetting that what you really want is love's confusing joy." Isn't what we really want love's confusing joy?

In the second real of the movie, we look inside our own hearts and allow the trajectory of our lives to move from inside out. In the second real of the movie, we own our neediness. We honor, instead of deny, what we need. What do we all need? Love. We all need love and acceptance.

We need love and acceptance. In the second real of the movie, we own our needs and get in touch with what has heart, meaning, and passion for us. In the second real of the movie, we move into a different psychological space, a different psycho-spiritual space. We're no longer concerned with controlling or manipulating other people. We want to be in the second real more and more. We want to be less controlling. This is the less that is more. It is more healthy, though not normal.

I once heard Robert Bly talk about [TITLE OF POEM] this wonderful poem William Blake wrote about relationships. Blake felt that there are four stages to relationship: "It's a fourfold vision I see; And a fourfold vision is given to me; Tis' fourfold in its supreme delight; And threefold in soft Beulah's night; And twofold always may God us keep from single vision and Newton's sleep." (Newton made the world predictable. He gave us the laws of classical mechanics, classical physics.) Predictability doesn't leave much room for the confusing joy of love.

There are four stages of relationships. As an example for the first stage of relationship, Bly uses a New York cabbie who says, "I look out for number one buddy." It's a little cold down there in stage number one.

The second stage of relationship is when we see ourselves in relationship to other people. We're in relationship with others, and, as good codependents, we can look out for them now as well. It's a little warmer there.

The third stage of relationship is Beulah. Beulah is the heat and fire of romantic passion. You come into number two and something happens—some spark ignites, and you fall in love. Remember what it's like when you have just fallen in love? Someone falls in love with you, and you can't believe it. It's really hot in number three. In fact, you're in heat for each other. Whenever you're together, you can't keep your hands off of each other. It's very intense.

Well, you can't stay there. That's Beulah. It's wonderful, but you can't stay there for five, ten, fifteen, or fifty years. It's not that you can't rekindle the embers. You can. But, let's face it, it's not the same.

So because normal isn't healthy, the tendency is to fall back out of number three, Beulah, into number two, and the lovers become more like companions. At this stage, when your companion is going to do something you want him or her to do, you're going to support it. When your companion is going to do something you don't want him or her to do, you won't support it.

"What do you mean I'm controlling?"

But there's the fourth stage of relationship. The fourth stage relationship is the alchemical, mystical union in which you support the creative impulse at work within your partner. If she's going to do something that has heart, meaning, and passion for her, you'll support her in her quest. Even if it isn't what you would chose for her script. You'll support it because she is honoring something that is coming out of her own center. It has heart, meaning, and passion for her. And even though it wouldn't be what you'd choose for her to do, you'll support her doing it because you love her in that fourth-stage way.

Healthy support is support of the creative impulse at work within others. I'll give you the poem again. "It's a fourfold vision I see; And a fourfold vision is given to me; Tis' fourfold in its supreme delight; And threefold in soft Beulah's night; And twofold always may God us keep from single vision in Newton's sleep."

I think Blake had something there. I think that the fourth stage of relationship happens in the second real when people honor what has heart, meaning, and passion for themselves, thereby honoring their own creative impulses. We have to have that relationship with ourselves before we can give healthy fourth-stage support to others. I'm not talking about the often distorted and limited view of Eros as the sexual form of love here, but, rather, Eros in the classic Greek sense.

In Greek mythology, Eros was responsible for creating life on earth. Passion came from Eros and is what draws us to explore the Fourth Pole. Robert Shelton wrote that passion "continues to pull one toward greater and deeper dimensions of experience. Some, including St. Augustine, have considered Eros to be what draws humans toward god."

Great. What does that mean in a relationship? It might mean somebody has a really solid, secure job, and they're making all this money, and if they go and pursue their passion they might not make so much money. In the first reel of the movie, we have many of Blake's second-stage relationships, full of "if" clauses. "If I get the new car, if I get this, and if I get that, then you can pursue your dream."

In the second real of the movie, there is no "if" clause in this scenario. When a partner is following her creative impulse, support is given. We encourage our partner to allow the creative impulse to give direction to the trajectory of her life. Here we see Blake's fourth-stage of relationship.

One way of talking about this material is to talk about how it compares with the Grail Quest. The Grail Quest, according to Joseph Campbell, who was interested in comparative mythology, represents the fundamental myth of western culture. The Grail was the cup used to collect the blood of Jesus on the cross, after he was stabbed in the side with a spear, or the cup that was passed at the Last Supper. Whether it exists as a religious artifact is controversial.

As a scientist, I tended to pooh-pooh mythology because it wasn't factual. Then I discovered that a myth is a story about something that never happened yet is happening all the time. There's a truth that's conveyed through the storyline even though the story is not factual.

King Author and the Knights of the Roundtable are all part of the Grail Quest mythology. About four main versions of the Grail Quest were written between the years 1180 and 1220, and these different versions share certain common elements.

At this point in history, in medieval in Europe, whatever you did with your life was totally determined by your inheritance. In other words, if you were born a surf, you begot surfs. If you were born a noble person, you begot noble people. If you were a peasant and got tired of living in the hut, with the animals, and went up to the big house, knocked on the door, and said, "You know, I'm really tired of living in squalor with the animals. I'd like to move in with you." Would that be well received?

No, you'd be told to get out of there. But the reverse is also true. If you were nobility and went down to the hut and said, "I'm tired of living in splendor, I want to live in squalor with you." You'd be told to get out and go back to where you belong. In medieval times, whatever you did was culture bound. You didn't marry who you fell in love with, you married whomever your family decided you should marry. Whatever you did with your life was totally determined by your inheritance.

What about the Knights of the Roundtable? Whatever a knight did was determined by the rules of conduct for knights. In other words, your behavior as a knight was determined by your training. Your training was part of your inheritance.

The myth has the knights sitting at the Roundtable. Why is the table round? Because everyone sitting there is of equal stature. Now, Arthur always liked to have an adventure before dinner. And one night this Grail appears veiled above the table. Parcival, piercer of the veil, stands up and says, "I vow to go on a quest after the Holy Grail to find it unveiled." He sits down, and everyone sups.

After they eat, Parcival goes off on his quest, and somewhere between five and twenty years later he finally comes to the Grail Castle. He goes in, and the Grail King is carried out on a stretcher to greet him. Parcival is moved by sympathy and compassion to ask the king what ails him. But he's been taught, by virtue of his inheritance, that knights don't ask questions. So he doesn't do what is in his own heart. He doesn't ask the king what ails him. He goes to bed that night, wakes up in the morning . . . and the castle is gone.

But the knight, by virtue of perseverance and determination, continues on his quest. Years later, once again, he finds the Grail Castle. The king is carried out. This time Parcival allows what's in his own heart to move him. He asks the king what ails him, and the quest succeeds. The knight returns home and is received as a hero.

So let's see how this myth ties in with what we've been discussing. In the first reel of the movie we get an inheritance. The culture is passed to us. We get acculturated. We are taught what's proper, to do what's proper. It wasn't proper for the knight to ask questions. Knights don't ask questions. At first, he did not honor what was in his heart. He did what was proper: What did Montagu, quoting Clifford, say about doing what's proper? It's not always right to do what's proper. It may not be a good thing.

The knight becomes a hero by taking the risk of breaking the rules of his own inheritance. He's not rebelling against anything. He's honoring his own needs. Feeling sympathy and compassion, what's in his own heart, is giving direction to his life. He returns home a hero because of the risk that he took in following his heart.

The way a knight goes on a quest is this: He enters the forest, under cover of darkness, alone, and in a place where there's no path. If he goes on a trail, it's somebody else's path. You make your own path on your quest and in your life. You lead your life, or you follow someone else's.

According to Campbell, going out on your own and making your way in the dark, led by what has heart for you, is the fundamental myth of western culture. I think this ties in to what we're talking about. The definition of hero is one who follows the path of courage. The root of the word courage is *coeur,* which means "heart" in French.

The hero's a person who follows the path of courage, of heart. For me to have the courage to break out of known patterns of response and to generate new healthier ones, I need to listen to my h-ear-t. It's not easy to do it by myself, though. I need the support of other people. This knight did it alone.

Well, that's who we tend to honor—the self-made men and women who accomplishe their quests alone. So sometimes, when we want to explore new paths, we have trouble asking for the support we need. I think we need to update the myth. I think we need a more modern myth, one that is inclusive of the importance of healthy support.

But, I think this myth, as is, is useful. We need to understand the value of discovering what has heart, meaning, and passion for us, and allow that to drive us. Otherwise, the scared one drives the engine of the psyche on the fuel of cultural norms. We spend our energy reacting out of our conditioning instead of taking direction from our heart center.

But I also think there are people who don't know what they love because they've been so focused on doing the right thing or doing what their parents or somebody else thought they should do. They don't really know what they want to do. If life is a movie, we have been encouraged to be an extra in everyone else's film. That's part of normal not being healthy.

But having the awareness that it's okay, better yet, healthy, to experiment in an effort at discovering your passion is a start. It's a step out of the box the environment built. It's okay to not know. In fact, there's a freedom there, but that freedom can be anxiety-provoking, stressful. You are entering the unknown, and it's scary. It's the forest without a path.

I'll give you a frog story I heard Coleman Barks tell. There are two frogs—an ocean frog and a pond frog. The meet by the latter's home. "Hey what's happening," says the ocean frog.

"Oh, not too much. Just hanging out having a lot of fun here at home," says the pond frog. "See, this is where I live," and he points to the pond, three feet by four feet by three feet. "Yeah, this is where I live. Hey look at this." He jumps in on one side, swims over, and jumps out the other side. "See. That's what it's like here where I live. Where do you live?"

The ocean frog says, "Well, I live in the ocean."

"The ocean? What's that like?"

"Well, you'll just have to come visit me sometime."

How would the ocean frog explain to the pond frog what it's like where he lives? He'll just have to go visit. We all have to go visit that larger world.

There is risk involved when you go on a quest, when you visit a larger world, but life can't be an adventure without risk. We are all star stuff. Move into the spotlight of your own attention. Be a star. That doesn't preclude other people from starring in the movie of their life. In fact, give yourselves a round of applause for taking a step. Inch-by-inch, life's a cinch, yard-by-yard, life is hard. While you're at it, give someone else a round of applause. Spread some good cheer because it's scary for other people too.

CHAPTER 12

OCEAN LUCK

Rumi was an ecstatic poet. He uses a metaphor of the ocean. Look at the poem at the beginning of Chapter 11. He uses the lines, "Praise the ocean, what we say a little ship, so the sea journey goes on, and who knows where, just to be held by the ocean is the best luck we could have. It's a total waking up. Why should we grieve that we've been sleeping. It doesn't matter how long we've been unconscious or groggy, but let the guilt go. Feel the motions of tenderness around you, the buoyancy."

In another poem, Rumi talks about ecstatic love being the ocean on which the Milky Way floats like a flake of foam on the sea. The Milky Way is our galaxy, our home. If ecstatic love is the ocean on which we float, we can easily take a dip in that ocean. Rumi describes the soul as having the shape of a bowl. All we have to do is dip our bowl and receive ecstatic love. Then Rumi reminds us to make sure the rim of our bowl stays moist by pouring ecstatic love into other people, by pouring it into our relationships. But we also need to make sure the rim stays moist on our side.

Part of what that means to me is that I don't have to be a generator. I don't have to generate the juice. It's not necessary that I generate wetness. All I have to do is empty and open. I need to empty out my egocentric concerns and not allow my fears to determine my behavior. Empty and open.

Frederick Beuchner has a great job as a writer and theologian. He doesn't have a church practice, but he's written more than a dozen wonderful books.

One really great book, called *Telling Secrets,* is about his own dysfunctional family. It's a wonderful book.

But he's also got a little book called, *Wishful Thinking: The ABCs of Theology.* He takes a letter of the alphabet and writes an essay on the subject that begins with that letter. There's one in there on *Healing,* in which he talks about imagining yourself as somewhat of a clogged up pipe. Imagine something is moving through you to other people. You don't have to feel particularly religious or spiritual or holy. Put your hands on somebody and let something move through you to them.

Because of our feelings of inadequacy, we can relate to being somewhat clogged up. But, you know, even a somewhat clogged up pipe can be used. Something can get through even a somewhat clogged up pipe. Who knows, maybe even part of that ocean.

We want to help others but feel we have to wait to feel good—unclogged—before we can be a healer. We think that once we unclog ourselves, we can really be a vessel for healing. After we become somehow more perfect, then we'll be useful. Don't wait. It's a con. If I hold in my awareness that I don't have to be the generator, I won't get burned out. If I don't have to be the generator, then I don't have to try so hard, push so hard. I don't have to do anything. I just empty and open.

How do I feel getting to serve in this way, allowing something to move through me to other people? I feel good, and I should. I'm holding the awareness of god in my attention. So, guess what I have energy for? Healing. But I don't have to be a generator. I just empty and open.

And ain't it great that we get to participate in our own little way? There's some benefit that we derive from this experience. When we fail to see the benefit, we burnout. In the first reel of the movie, we see ourselves as having to be the generator. We look upon our service as work we do for others. And then, when someone doesn't appreciate our service, our working our butts off, we are resentful. We don't enjoy the ride, the buoyancy, the motions of tenderness.

CHAPTER 13

MADE IN THE IMAGE

There's a Greek Orthodox saying, *cunna nase cunesu*. It means, "I must extend my hand to take God's hand," which means there's a part that I have to play. When I think about that, I recognize that I cannot be passive. There is some action for me to take. If I take the initiative, I get help. If I ask people in my support system for help, I get it. Why wouldn't that also be true of my relationship with God?

If I ask to be forgiven, I'm forgiven. I don't get a sign. There isn't something in the mailbox. I don't get writing on the wall. But if I ask for help, remembering to try to be of service, I think I get it.

Janis Joplin was a great singer. She had a tongue-in-cheek song about asking the Lord for a Mercedes Benz. When I think about asking and getting, I think about what I need that can't be denied. And what do I need? In the second real of the movie, we've established that we need love and acceptance. Another word for that is mercy. I need mercy. And when I ask for mercy, it has to be given.

Ever heard of the book *Finnigan's Wake*, kind of a famous book, written by James Joyce? The numbers eleven and thirty-two keep coming up over and over. Joseph Campbell wrote a book called *A Skeleton Key to Finnigan's Wake*, in which he interprets all the symbolism of this animal allegory. He also interprets the numbers eleven and thirty-two for the reader.

About five years after he wrote his book explaining all the symbolism of the Joyce book, he was teaching a class on early Christianity. He was preparing for the class and reading Romans and he came to the passage, "God you created us to be disobedient so that you could show us your mercy." He ran his finger across the page, and the passage was Romans 11:32. And he had this *ah ha* experience. *That's* what Joyce was talking about! Campbell was a Joyce scholar. He knew Joyce well and knew that Joyce was going to give god the full measure of his disobedience and receive the full measure of his mercy.

I think we're made to miss the mark, to lose our way, to forget what is important, and to be disobedient. We are made to sin, or whatever you want to call it. That's our nature. That's the way we're wired. And maybe we're wired that way so that God can have opportunities to show us that God exists. So when we ask for mercy, we can't be denied. We can't be denied. That's what I think about when I hear the phrase "ask and you shall receive."

How do you know you get mercy? You don't, necessarily. It's not measurable. But it's not nothing. I may feel something, but it's really a matter of faith. That's part of my belief system. And it's a great stress management tool.

Fear is the driver of the stress response. Driven by fear I want to feel safe. The safety of material things is not enough. I need to feel soul safe, safe in my center. Mercy is that safety net for me. Some people say, "Well I prayed to God for money, and I won the lottery." I don't think God has much to do with that. That's just my own belief, and we're limited by our own beliefs. I don't think God is moving things around like pieces on a chessboard. That's just my bias.

But I think we get help. I know I get help. Thank God.

"Just to be held by the ocean is the best luck we could have."

How can we ground what we're talking about in a practical way to our relationships and relational intelligence? Do you know how it feels to be around

161

people who have certain character flaws that really grate on you? You just don't like being around people like that, whatever the 'like that' happens to be. I had this same experience with Bob, a business associate. Our agreement went sour., and the way he handled the situation totally put me off. I just saw him as being unbelievably greedy.

It doesn't matter what the flaw in the other is. The point is that the feeling tone we carry is not good. Sometimes we have trouble doing the loving and accepting thing when we feel like the other person is a stinking, greedy pig.

Ever heard this expression: We're made in the image of God? Does God have a beard? Y chromosome? Two X's? What does that mean -- made in the image of God? Joe Campbell uses an analogy that I think is useful. It ties back into the psychological idea of the shadow. He talks about how the sun is related to the moon. I'll just extrapolating on that model.

The sun is all radiant, all light. What about the moon? The moon reflects the light of the sun and has its radiant aspect.

What is on the other side? Darkness. The other side is the dark side of the moon. So one way to see us is as the moon in relationship to the sun, or as the human in relationship to the evolutionary intelligence, or god. We have our radiant side and our dark side, the shadow. The shadow side of my personality has a whole lot of negative traits, traits I don't want to accept about myself. In this case, greediness.

I didn't want to accept the fact that I can be greedy, using the example of the experience that I had. I had this problem dealing with my own greediness, so I was projecting my shadow onto my business associate. I think this guy is greedy, but I don't think his greediness is what gets to me. What do you think gets me? What do you think causes me discomfort? He carries a flaw that I have, a flaw that I'm in denial about, a flaw that I don't want to deal with it. So I project it onto him.

He's reflecting back to me what I'm trying to hide. He is carrying it there for me. He's reflecting it right back, and I don't like how it feels. Because I haven't accepted that part of me, I project it onto him. I endarken him with my shadow. But in reality, I am the one in the dark.

Now, if I don't like how I'm feeling around someone, what can I do? I can name the flaw in this person. What is the flaw that I don't like? Greed. Then, what can I do? First, I accept that I'm greedy, too. Then I can eat the shadow. This is soul food.

Soul food is not only hominy grits and collard greens. Soul food is eating your own shadow. I can name the flaw in the other, and then I can name the flaw as my own.

My stream of consciousness flows like this: "Oh, I guess I haven't dealt with my own greediness. Here I've been so judgmental and so critical of this guy. I've been talking to other people about what a creep he is because he's so greedy." When I eat some soul food, I create humility. Being humble I can then ask for what I need to feel okay. Being humble I come back into a right relationship with this Mystery and ask for what I need. And if I ask, I receive.

I have to be given mercy because this is the way I was made. I'm not all light. I'm made in the image of this light, but I carry a shadow. And because that's the way I'm made—when I ask, I've got to be given mercy: love and acceptance. When I'm having trouble remembering to ask for mercy, when I'm lost, when I'm asleep, and when I don't like how I'm feeling, my observer "I" is closed. I need to open that "I," and watch myself, to discover why I'm feeling so stressed around Bob.

Stress is often connected back to relationships. What is the flaw that I see in the other person? Is it a flaw I carry? Is it a flaw I haven't integrated into my awareness? In answering those questions, my feeling tone brings me to a place where I can honor what I need. My feelings, especially when uncomfortable, can guide me back to right relationship. In that way, our feelings are sacred, even the ones we don't like.

How can I use my beliefs, my highest values, to support that process? Even if I'm functioning in the dynamic of the first reel of the movie, I can use my feeling tone; I can use how I'm feeling as a wake-up call. The discomfort I have in the psyche is there to get me to see what those feelings are about. The emphasis is on see. I have to be awake in order to see, and I can't be awake if the observer "I" is closed.

What is there to learn from this? In a sense, it serves me. It serves me developmentally. Isn't that interesting? I can be greedy. Owning the fact that I can be greedy, I can watch that part of me. Energy follows attention. What I pay attention to, I have energy for. When I shine the flashlight of my attention on my greedy part, I have energy to change.

It's the observer effect. I can act with awareness. I can recognize when I'm being greedy and keep that greedy part of me from expressing itself. It's the difference between repression and suppression. If I don't accept the idea that I can be greedy, I repress that and then project it onto others. In this case, Bob. If I accept the fact that I can be greedy, I can suppress that greedy part of me so that it doesn't contaminate my behavior.

Rumi says that straying maps the path. When I stray, when I miss the mark, I have an opportunity to take a step in the direction of emotional maturity. William Menninger, M.D., came up with seven criteria for emotional maturity:

- the ability to deal constructively with reality
- the capacity to adapt to change
- a relative freedom from symptoms that are produced by tensions and anxieties
- the capacity to find more satisfaction in giving than receiving
- the capacity to relate to other people in a consistent manner with mutual satisfaction and helpfulness
- the capacity to sublimate, to direct one's instinctive hostile energy into creative and constructive outlets
- the capacity to love

Five of the seven of these criteria talk about having the capacity to do something. Having the capacity doesn't mean that we always express that capacity. Straying maps the path. Straying gives us the opportunity to express our potential for healthy behavior.

Looking past the flaw in Bob, I can have not only sympathy and compassion but can also make a new, more positive connection with him. In that way, I'm exercising some of these capacities. It doesn't matter if you have a capacity if you don't exercise it. The stress in our relationship helps me tap my potential for change. I'm taking a step in my personal evolution toward emotional maturity. Accepting my shadow nature, accepting myself with my flaws, I then am more accepting of other people with their flaws. I can then have a healthier relationship with Bob without Bob changing, and my highest values support that work.

And what I'm doing is changing myself. I'm becoming more and more myself. Becoming who we are is part of our evolution. We are most at ease, most comfortable, when we are ourselves.

But is that what we see people do? What does a politician try to do? A politician is trying to get the vote. Politicians really bug us because they're chameleons; they just say whatever they need to say to get the vote. But our politicians are a reflection of the collective consciousness. In a sense, our politicians, the leadership of our country, are mirroring back to the country itself. We are collectively projecting our own codependent, inauthentic nature onto them, and they show it right back to us on a big screen TV.

In the first reel in the movie of our lives, to make up for our feelings of inadequacy, we project something to others that compensates, so they see us adequate. In a sense, we're looking to get the vote. We want them to give us an "A" for adequate. So guess what we get to do if we want better politicians? We have to change ourselves. Elect yourself.

Ghandi said, "The task of a government should be to work for the liberation and elevation of each individual." We can't expect the government to do that unless we first free ourselves.

CHAPTER 14

THE SACRED ONE

Earlier we talked about the feather effect, and how one more thing added to the well-loaded psyche can cause us to decompensate. I think the reverse of that's also true. How can we lighten each other's load? You have a conversation with someone at work and they say something to you and you think, *wow!* A light bulb goes on and now you know what you're going do at that presentation or say at that meeting. And you wonder how did that work?

The Dalai Lama talked about the three Rs: respect for self, respect for others, and responsibility for all our actions. What if we were conscious of the quality of the energy we send to other people, so that what we sent to other people all the time was respectful and positive? What would our days be like if we took responsibility for carrying and sending this respect? What would work be like? What would our families be like?

In the last chapter, we talked about how we're made in the image of god. "Made in the image of" means that we reflect the light of the mysterious parent. But, we also have our shadow. And we discussed how we project our shadow, which contains what we might consider to be character flaws, onto other people. We talked about how we endarken other people. And earlier on we talked about how we all have feelings of inadequacy and about how we tend to use the wonderfulness, the radiance, of other people to reinforce our feelings of inadequacy.

When we compare ourselves with the radiant, we're schmucks. Well, just as we couldn't see the flaw in the other unless we carried it ourselves, we couldn't see the radiance of another, if we weren't radiant also. It isn't just that we project the shadow; we also project the light. And we get to choose what we look for in others. If we look for the flaws we find them. And if we look for the radiance, we find it. We get to decide. What do you want to look for in other people?

Earlier on we talked about how we all have a scared one we never get rid of. And when we travel to the Fourth Pole, into the hub, we see the scared one projecting compensatory images out to the surface of life, so we're seen as adequate. But that is not all of what we are. There were two birds sitting on that selfsame tree.

If you transpose the letters c and a in scared, what are you left with? Sacred. We not only have a scared one, we also have a sacred one inside, in our sacred center, in our heart of hearts. And that's the paradox. We have both. We are both.

The sacred one has limitless possibilities for growth and development. When we stop being paranoid and defensive about our inadequacies, the energy available to us is enormous. When we let go of our concern for our image in the eyes of others, we discover how much energy we were wasting. We plug the energy leak and energy becomes available for the huge foolish projects Rumi talked about. We tap into a reservoir or, better yet, a stream, a flow of something life-giving, nourishing, potent.

Deep within each of us is a radiant core that we can mine. When we tap into this mine, we may at times look foolish to others. But this ore we bring forth is not fool's gold. It is the real thing.

This knowledge of the paradoxical nature of the human psyche allows us to operate through awareness. With awareness, no interaction with another is aimed at reinforcing feelings of inadequacy—in ourselves or in others. To the contrary, the energy exchange is aimed at connecting to the sacred one, at creating a psychological and social space for the expression of giftedness.

Remember what Goethe said and what our best teachers did with us: "Treat people as they are and they remain that way. Treat them as though they were what they are capable of becoming, and you will help them move toward . . . that which they are capable of becoming."

ROARING TIGERS

Tiger, Tiger burning bright

In the forest of the night.

What immortal hand or eye

Did frame thy fearful symmetry?

--William Blake

The sacred one is the luminous aspect of our humanness. The sacred component is not a product of conditioning. It is not burdened with egocentric vision. It is, however, often covered by psychological brushwood. The scared one is in hiding; the sacred one is hidden—so deeply hidden sometimes that we may not believe it exists.

I want to tell you a tiger story that will help clear away some of the brushwood. This is an ancient story, one I heard Joseph Campbell tell. I won't presume his skill as a raconteur, but this story is one I'll always remember.

A pregnant tigress is on the prowl hungry for goat. She comes to a clearing and spots a herd of goats grazing at a distance. She stealthily slips up on the herd and picks out her prey. Slowly, she moves in for the kill and suddenly leaps upon her victim. But while she is in midair, the goat changes position so that when she lands on her prey, two sharp goat horns pierce her heart. At the moment of contact, she sustains a mortal wound and lies dying in the grass.

The traumatized goat is dazed, yet very aware of the closeness of the call. He just saw his little goat life flash before his eyes. He can hardly believe he's not badly injured when he notices the spectacle.

In her dying moments, the pregnant tiger's uterus begins to contract, and she delivers a beautiful little tiger cub.

The goat is amazed at the miracle. Out of this death comes new life. He thinks, "Wow! What a beautiful little tiger cu . . .b . . . Wait a minute! That's a tiger. I'm a goat. Tigers eat goats. This is a problem."

So the young goat goes to get the goat elders. They come over to investigate the situation. "Let's see now. That's a tiger. We're goats. Tigers eat goats. Yep, it's a problem. But, hey, wait a minute. She doesn't know she's a tiger. Why don't we just raise her like a goat. She'll eat goat food instead of goat. Yeah, that's the ticket. She'll live a goat life with the herd. She'll live like us and be like us. Sure, it'll work."

Time passes, and it's as the elders said it would be. The little tigress lives a goat life eating goat food instead of goat and moves as one with the herd. Things go along smoothly. The tigress isn't growing into her full, mature tiger self because she's eating grass instead of goat, and her true identity remains hidden.

One day, a large female tiger comes along hungry for goat. She catches the scent of the herd and tracks them down. She begins to select her prey when she notices a tiger grazing with the herd.

Astonished at what she's witnessing, the tigress forgets about her hunger and runs out from cover to satisfy her curiosity. The herd dashes away, but the large mature tigress is much faster than the goat-tiger and catches her easily.

"What the heck are you doing out here with these goats?" she asks. Don't you know you're a tiger and that tigers eat goats?"

The young tigress looks up at the mature one and says, "Baaaah, Baaaah.."

The big tiger cannot believe her ears. "What! That's not what tigers say. Tigers say, GRRRRRRR! GRRRRRRR!"

And her booming roar blasts the little one's ears back. But all she can muster is another "Baaaah, Baaaah."

No matter what the mature tigress does, she cannot convince the young one of her true tiger nature. Until finally she spots a quiet pool of water nearby. She moves over to drink and sees her image reflecting up to her. She calls the young one over and says, "Here, put your head here next to mine above the pond. Now, do you see those eyes, those whiskers, those stripes?"

"Stripes! What? Can it be?" thought the little goat-tiger. In an instant the truth was revealed.

"You are a tiger like me. You are meant to live a different life than the one you have known. Come with me," said the tigress.

And off they went to live their tiger lives.

171

Do you see the problem? We are all born tigers and taught to be goats. We live our goat lives, eating goat food and moving with the herd. We feel inadequate and easily let others "get our goat." Or, to compensate for our feelings of inadequacy, we become a bully and "billy" other goats.

The story then reveals the dynamics we have been discussing: the scared one bleating out anxious tones from a fearful hiding spot, or the big one picking on other, smaller goats to establish dominance. Reinforcing the feelings of inadequacy in others, the bully reveals his secret. He is unaware of his *modus operandi* until a still larger one appears and his tail drops between his legs I submission to the new alpha figure.

The scared one/big one and the goat are synonymous. We all have a scared one inside, but it is not our whole nature. Early on we are imprinted to think goat thoughts and to move with the herd. We replicate ourselves and teach our children to do the same. But there is this other one, this tiger self, this essential self that waits to be discovered.

"Tiger, Tiger, burning bright," is our luminous sacred one, who is hidden behind the conditioning of a lifetime.

"What immortal hand or eye did frame thy fearful symmetry?"

When our sacred one remembers, re-members, reconnects to the sacred set of parents that birthed a universe, look out!

Because we have feelings of inadequacy doesn't mean we're inadequate. Because we have fears, doesn't mean we can't face them to see what they have to teach us. For, it may be only in facing what we fear the most that we discover our true stripes. GRRRRRR!

We experience our core "burning bright" and this light illuminates a new way. The familiar is seen with a new sense of possibility. Our confusion gives way to a brief moment of clarity. We see through the illusion of who we thought we were to live for an instant what we actually are.

And that moment, that one instant of direct knowing, also reveals to us who is hidden within everyone else. And though we cannot hold that moment, its memory holds us, enfolds us. It informs all we do henceforth the moment we remember because our energy follows attention.

Hey you! Yeah you! What are you paying attention to? Are you busting your butt trying to keep up with the herd? Exhausting, isn't it? Your energy follows your attention. What you pay attention to, you have energy for.

If you pay attention to your true tiger nature, you will have the energy for living out your true tiger life. In those moments, you become a metaphorical pond for others to see their true reflection in the deep pools of your tiger eyes.

CHAPTER 15

SERVICE

I want to tell you the story of Evy McDonald. Evy was a nurse in 1980 at a hospital intensive care unit. She ran both the surgical and the medical intensive care units. Then she got sick and ended up in the medical intensive care unit herself, as a patient. Evy had this strange problem, and the doctors couldn't figure out right away what was wrong with her.

Her body just quit working. Different systems started shutting down. The doctor was trying to talk her into going on a respirator when the neurologist, who'd been working her up, came in to giver her the diagnosis. Actually, he walked in the room, stood at her bedside, looked out the window, and said, "Well Evy, our worst fears have been confirmed. It is ALS—Lou Gehrig's disease. As you know, it's an incurable disease and because, in your case, it's onset was so rapid, you probably only have about six months to live. I'm so sorry."

He never looks at Evy and leaves the room. Why doesn't he look at Evy? He can't do much by way of treating her. There's no "fix" for her. So it brings up all his own feelings of inadequacy. He can't cure her, and he doesn't know how to deal with that reality. So, she doesn't even have the warmth of his own gaze to comfort her when she hears this devastating news. But he's probably doing the best job he can with the information he got about how to do doctor. You don't want to get emotionally involved. You want to hold on to your objectivity. Life is a terminal condition for all patients. They're all going to die so don't get too close.

He leaves the room, and Evy is in a state of shock. She's just gotten a death sentence. To make a story short, Evy decides that if she's only got six months to live, she's going to make them the best six. She does a timeline of her life.

She looks at her development physically, mentally, emotionally, and spiritually. Physically, she saw herself as fat. She also she had contractures of an arm and leg secondary to having polio as a child. She had been in an iron lung in her youth, but she was as cut as a button and was a polio poster child. That was the physical part.

Mentally, she was a powerhouse. This was the result of her rebellion to her third grade teacher, who told her, "Evy, with your handicap, you know you'll always be taken care of. You don't have to worry about this academic material. In fact, you shouldn't even be at this school. You should be over at the Omaha school for the mentally and physically handicapped." That broke Evy's heart.

But, by golly she was going to show that teacher. She was going to prove how adequate she was. She won the spelling bee, the oratory contest, became the best student in her class. That remained true throughout her school years. She graduated as valedictorian of her high school class. She went off to college, did well, and went on to nursing school, where she graduated at the top of her class. She went on to get a master's degree in nursing. She was a mental powerhouse.

But when Evy looked at her emotional life, she saw a lot of depression. She was so depressed in high school, she drove her car off the side of a road hoping to hit a tree and never wake up. But she made a mistake. She missed the tree. It's amazing how our mistakes can actually serve us at times. It's an interesting dynamic. She was really good at what she did, but how did she feel about herself? Not so good.

To Evy, spirituality was connected to service. The idea of service, of putting something into action, was a form of spirituality for her. It was more meaningful than simply saying she had certain spiritual beliefs. Her whole life had been committed to service. As a teenager, she was a candy striper at the local hospital. She asked the head of volunteer services what was the most number of hours any candy striper had ever served in a year. Evy smashed the record and was awarded a little plaque.

She then examined her intentions behind her service more closely. She divided all the service she'd done into two categories: type one and type two. She referred to type one service as R & R, service done for reward or recognition. She saw type two service as service done out of a sense of duty. So her whole life she'd been committed to service, but all the service was either type one or type two.

Evy decided that for the last six months of her life that she still wanted to be involved in service. But it would have to be another kind of service. Evy wanted to be involved with what she called type three service. Type three service, interestingly enough, had to do with love and acceptance. That's what she wanted to do. She didn't want to serve for reward or recognition or out of some sense of duty. She wanted to serve in a way that was loving and accepting. She wanted to serve in a way that met her own needs. But Evy had a problem. Evy hadn't fully loved and accepted herself.

So Evy looked daily in the mirror at her naked self. She sat there in a wheelchair and saw all these negative attributes in her reflection. She wrote them down and began to work through all her negativity so she could get to the place where she could finally love and accept the person looking back, flaws and all. Then she took that love and acceptance and she gave it away, indiscriminately, to everyone she met. She didn't give it to make somebody feel better, out of a sense of duty, or for a reward or recognition. She gave it away because she wanted to feel better herself.

She was selfish, in a way, because she owned what she needed. Then, she gave away what she needed to other people. We all need love an acceptance. And the mystery is, when you give away love, guess what? You know the expression "go to the well"? If you put a bucket in a well and you bring up water, does the level of the well go down when a bucket of water is removed? No. Because the water table immediately replaces what was taken.

So you take out a bucket of water and there's more of it. Love is like that. When we give it away we are not diminished. When we give love, we get more of it. So Evy was giving away love and acceptance to everyone, and she had her best six months. ... And another six.... And another six.... And another.... And another.... And another.... And.... Evy Macdonald is one of the first people in the world to be cured of ALS—Lou Grehig's disease.

Evy did what she did to feel better and to have her best six months, not to get rid of ALS. It's an incurable disease. She knew that. What she was trying to do was make the most of the short amount of time she had to live. But in so doing, something happened that's very instructive for all of us.

I think Evy's story is a new version of an old tale. Aren't we here to serve? I think we're here to serve. We're here to make it a little better than it was before we got here. We're not here simply to replicate the status quo. How can we serve others in a way that serves us? I think we have to own our neediness. Evy was, in a certain way, selfish. Maybe selfish isn't so bad. Maybe it's okay to own what our needs are and give away what we need. It is a new version of an old story.

Two thousand years ago, a teacher gives a wonderful talk. A lot of people are in the audience. And at the end of the talk, they're hungry. There are a couple of people present who have some food, some bread and fish, to be specific. The teacher goes over and says, "You know these people are hungry. I want you to feed them." And the one with the food says, "There won't be enough food for all these people." And what does the speaker say? "Trust me on this. Just give it away." Okay, I don't think that story is really about bread and fish. But I think it's a wonderful metaphor.

Giving away this kind of food, love, and acceptance to other people is something that doesn't require medical training. In fact, it probably doesn't require spiritual training. We don't have to pass a test. We can self select, "elect" ourselves, and decide to put it in our job description as a human being. What I want is to be more loving and accepting. Being religious isn't required.

Speaking of religion, that reminds me of a humorous story. I have a friend named Milton Friedman, who was a speechwriter for the Ford administration. This is his story. You may know of another Milton Friedman, a very famous economist. Sometimes people get them confused. One day, my friend gets a call from a church in California that has all these excess funds. They didn't know what to do with the money and thought that Milton Freedman, the famous economist, might be able to give them some good counsel.

So the church calls, "Is this Milton Freedman?"

"Yes."

"Well, we're a church with all these excess funds. What would you advise us to do with this money?"

"Have you thought of giving it to the poor?"

Pause. "Is this the real Milton Freedman?"

"Yes. Is this a real church?"

Okay, what if we don't have money to give? What can we do for the poor? Give of ourselves. Most of us are always complaining about how screwed up the world is, and the media daily affirms our beliefs lest we forget. Take a marker sometime and circle all the positive stories on the front page of the newspaper. That marker will last a long time. If the world is really screwed up then there's no shortage of opportunity to serve. There's no shortage of places to do something positive.

And you don't have to look very far to do it. Sometimes it can be as close as the person in the mirror. You deserve a break today, so go out and say hurrah. Living our McNormal lives, don't we deserve a break today? I think we do, but I don't think it's a Big Mac. I think what we need in the way of a break today is: love, acceptance, kindness, and warm compassion.

In spite of our flaws, in fact, all the more so, because of them, we need love and acceptance. I don't want to wait for ALS to help me grow, mature, and develop into what I potentially am. I want to use the little stressors that come up in my daily living for all they're worth. I don't want to wait for a big, catastrophic event to rock my world: a heart attack or cancer, a sick child, or an accident. I don't want to wait.

Stories like Evy's inspire me. Just knowing she is out there doing this work is a source of encouragement for me. I can be selfish too. If I'm serving because of what I derive from the service I give, there's no reason to be ego-inflated behind the service I give. I'm not doing it for someone else, I'm doing it for me.

It reminds me of a story, a short story. Two people are walking down the street when a beggar approaches asking for money. One person reaches in his pocket and gives some change to the beggar. The other person says, " You shouldn't do that for them. It only encourages them." The first person replies, "I'm not doing it for them. I'm doing it for me."

Rabindranath Tagore wrote the following the poem:

"I lived on the shady side of the road and watched
my neighbor's gardens across the way reveling
in the sunshine.
I felt I was poor and from door-to-door went with
My hunger.
The more they care me from their careless abundance
The more I became aware of my beggar's bowl.
Till one morning I awoke from my sleep at the
Sudden opening of my door, and you came and
Asked for holms.
In despair I broke the lid of my chest open and
Was startled into finding my own wealth."

For most of her life, Evy put herself third. If we're going to put ourselves third, how do we do it in a healthy way? That's good question.

I have the idea that before we're born, we have this audience with God. And God says, "Well, kid you're going to be born pretty soon. Now, I'm going to start you out as a tiny little thing in a hot tub. It'll be really warm in there, about 98.6 degrees. Everything you need will be right there in the hot tub. You'll grow and mature and develop in there.

Everything will be going along fine and then something kind of weird happens after seven months or so. You will find yourself turned upside down in the hot tub, and you won't be able to put yourself right side up again. And then your quarters will get more and more cramped. You'll hardly be able to move your unit. And then after about nine months or so, another really weird thing happens. Someone comes and pulls the plug on the hot tub. The water goes out, and you're left high and dry.

And then another really strange thing that happens. It's like an earthquake occurs, and you will find your head jammed down the drain of the hot tub. And your face will be all smashed. And your shoulders will be squished together, and you won't be able to move anything. And someone will put their hands on your head. Yank you into a cold, brightly lit room and go, "Wham!" And that's what it's like to be born.

Now, the woman bringing you into the world will be suffering through something called birthing pains. To birth something new into the world there is often pain. But she'd gladly suffer those pains to have you, this new life, in her life. Now your mission, should you choose to accept it, is—amidst the pain and suffering and unfairness of the world—to discover who you really are as my child. Remember Me. And then come home.

So, how do we put God first? Maybe to do that is to risk being who we really are as a child of that Mystery. So first we have to be ourselves, to put everybody else second, and to put our own egocentric concerns third. It may be that other people will see us as selfish, but that's a risk worth taking. It is also what our highest values call upon us to do.

About two thousand years ago, that same teacher we talked about earlier started this healing ministry with very powerful medicine. Blind people could see, lame people could walk, and he was even able to raise people from the dead. Word of this healer spread, and people brought themselves and their infirm family members to be made well by this healer. Then, with very little warning, the healer disappears. He goes on a desert retreat for forty days.

You can imagine what those who had come to be healed thought about him leaving them when they had such need. And you can imagine they were probably saying derogatory words about his lack of consideration for their problems. In fact, they probably said, "What's wrong with him, leaving us in the lurch? How selfish."

After the teacher returns from the desert, he gives his gift. The gift that is the reason we talk about him two thousand years later. If he would have stayed with the infirm and not honored his own needs, the world would not be talking about him now.

When we are doing what is healthy for us, when we are honoring our needs, our sacred one, other people may wonder what's wrong with us. They may see us as selfish. Yet it is only by honoring our own needs that we discover our gifts. And our gifts, once discovered, can then be used in the service of the common good. And we are here to serve.

If we risk being who we REALLy are capable of being, instead of just being who we've been programmed to be by the culture, we may serve in a way that's mutually beneficial. Putting ourselves third means putting our egocentric concerns last—like our image in the eyes of other people. If that healer had been concerned with his image, he never would have gone into the desert.

Remember the lines from the Rumi poem about Noah? "Go start some huge foolish project like Noah. It makes absolutely no difference what people think of you." Imagine what Noah's thinking. *What? A boat? Two of every animal? Ah, excuse me sir, but I haven't discovered my boat-builder self yet.* Do you think he thought he could make a boat? Yet that's what god put in Noah's INbox, along with a once-in-the-history-of-the-planet deadline.

What are we capable of? I don't know. But we might surprise ourselves. I mentioned my friend and mentor Don Campbell earlier. He asked one of his mentors, "How do you know when you're doing God's will?"

His mentor replied, "You'll be having the time of your life, and there will be plenty of surprises along the way."

Another friend and mentor, George O'Laughlin, and I were talking about this same subject once. He told me a story about a homily a priest gave about god's will. How do you know when you're doing god's will? He said to look to your gifts. God's will is in there hiding.

Life will test us all, whether in the desert, with a boat in our INbox, or a deadline at work. And in response to that INput, we may discover what allows us to be truly ourselves in a way we never thought we were capable. It may force us to go to the Fourth Pole and see how love and fear can both be used to help us discover our true nature.

THE DOOR

Where Jesus lives, the great-hearted gather

We are a door that is never locked.

If you are suffering any kind of pain,

Stay near that door.

Open it!

Rumi

A door is an interesting metaphor. It separates, and it connects. Let's go through that door that we are and see what's required for us to better serve. Stephen Mitchell says that compassion is equal to our love touching the suffering of another person, whereas pity occurs when our fear touches the suffering of another. The scared one feels pity; the sacred one feels compassion. In the first reel of the movie, we're driven by fear; in the second real, driven by love, we discover what it means to be compassionate.

We are here to serve. We are here to serve the suffering community. How do we joyfully participate in the suffering of the world? We can't do that when our connection is made through fear. Fear connects us, but not joyfully.

What I would like to do is use another ontological model, another developmental model, to view us afresh. Or, as is actually the case, take an ancient model and fold into our post-modern reality.

As a needy person, I need a lot of help. And Joseph Campbell has helped with my understanding of the model. Without going back and researching his very words, I will reconnect synaptically and energetically with his interpretation of the chakras and their role in our psychosocial, spiritual growth.

The model has seven stages of development moving from the base, animal impulses through the personal, rational into the transrational. The energetic centers have been called *chakras* in the system of Kundalini Yoga.

The first chakra is at the 'root base' of the spine and is associated with the anus. When a human being is functioning at this level, his psychological system is behaviorism. He functions in the world as B. F. Skinner described. Skinner said that the human being is nothing but behavior in response to environment. There is no interior being yearning for freedom. There is no free will. We imprint, then we are conditioned to be like those who conditioned us, through pleasure and pain.

Skinner later changed his thinking. I heard him interviewed when his autobiography came out, and he said, "If what I believe is true of the human condition, then the title of my autobiography should be 'the autobiography of a non-person.' "

Campbell said that the animal that represents this stage of development is the snake, which he referred to as a 'traveling esophagus.' We eat and defecate. We function at the lowest level of survival, the belly's hunger being the primary urge. That means there's not much happening at this level in the way of compassion and community.

The second chakra is associated with the genitals. When we bring our energy up to this center, we visit 'her favorite resort,' Campbell's translation from the original Sanskrit.

Our psychological system is Freudian, and the primary driver of the engine of the psyche is the sexual impulse. Personal survival is a beginning, but survival of the species is dependent upon procreation. Here, our energy is directed toward satisfying this personal urge, which, as a side effect, supplies recruits to replace us, and the species, when we succumb to the 'death wish.'

The third chakra is centered in the region of the solar plexus. Here the movement of the individual is still very much outer directed. The ego is activated to supply food for self and young. So that we may live other living things must die. Life feeds on life. The psychological system is Adlerian, the will to power is driving the psyche. We establish dominance by competition and it is survival of the fittest.

The lower three chakras are all concerned with our animal, human animal, development. We can't deny those aspects of our nature, but if we function only from these three centers, we will never fully celebrate them or unfold our psychosocial spiritual tents on higher ground.

Service, compassion, and community are higher order processes, and their expression in these psychological systems is rudimentary and survival-oriented. Survival is not enough. It is a beginning. Living fully into that which we are capable of takes a quantum leap with the opening of the fourth chakra—the door.

The fourth chakra is represented by the region of the heart. It is referred to as the heart chakra. When our energy rises to or enters this space, our metaphorical heart opens. We open to life in a way that is uniquely human. When this occurs, we are born again. In a metaphorical sense, we *are* born again. We see with new eyes, hear with new ears, feel with new sensors (nerves), and think with a new perspective that is inclusive of the transrational.

We understand what love is at a level that is non-controlling and unconditional. When our hearts open and we resonate at this frequency, animal survival becomes secondary. Schopenhauer, Campbell reminds us, wondered what it is that moves in us that would cause us to yield our lives for someone we have never even met? There is something embedded in the human being that spontaneously drives people to jump in the icy Potomac River to rescue strangers in a plane accident. What is that mystery?

It is not logical. The scared one can't hold us back because safety is no longer paramount. Our own survival becomes secondary. It is not because of a 'death wish,' as Freud would like us to believe. Rather, it is a 'life wish.' In that moment, the life of another is more important than our own. Not simply some special person's life, but any person's life.

When the heart opens, we become inclusive. Remember the poem, "He drew a circle that left me out. But love and I had wit to win. We drew a circle that brought him in"? At this stage, we bring into our circle of community everyone, even our enemies.

"Love your enemies," Jesus said. He didn't say like your enemies. Being able to love someone and not like them is the kind of lunacy we become capable of—the kind of craziness that leads us past the limited, though logical, view of the ego into reconciliation. The idea of serving the community really becomes alive to the extent that it is inclusive. And the limits of our former, tribal conditioning melt away in the light of the open heart.

We grew up with the psychology of scarcity about love. It was as if we had a finite amount of it, and we held it close to our hearts, only giving it to those who had tribal affiliation. But we misperceived the mystery of love. We can't think about love with the psychology of scarcity. Love requires the psychology of abundance. As we mentioned above, when you give it away you have more of it.

When the fourth chakra is opened, compassion's healing power can flow through us to others—that is Evy's type three service. The energetic connection bonds the sufferer and the compassionate one. Having come together in unity, community is established at a deeper level.

Campbell said that you could look at the upper three chakras as mirror images of the lower three.

First Reel--Fear   Door   Second Real—Love

Heart   4   Chakra

3   5

2   6

1   7

The fifth chakra is a mirror of the third. It is located at the throat and opens after the heart door opens. Here our energy is inner directed as distinct from its mirror, the ego-centered, outer-directed third. The ego is often concerned with forcing its will upon the outer world. Once the fifth chakra is opened, we direct that aggressive energy at our own ego. I check my own ego. With my ego in check, I can serve the common good of the community much better. Service, in fact, becomes the driver.

The sixth chakra is represented by the third eye. It is an mirror of the second, our sexual center. When the third eye opens, we see the Beloved in all things. All interactions with others in our community become an opportunity to commune with the Beloved. All sexual coupling is tantric yoga, union with the Beloved.

The seventh chakra is at the crown or just above the crown of the head. When the crown opens, there is no other. There is only the ONE. It's mirror is the first . When the seventh opens, that which we eat is that which we are. There is no separation.

Our ability to serve the evolutionary intelligence increases with our psychosocial, spiritual development. Our ability to express compassion and experience community increases as we evolve on the one hand and forget on the other. Once a center opens we have a direct experience of that level of awareness. But, we don't stay open. We forget.

Then, by forgetting, we may become the one in need of the healing power of compassion and community. Our suffering may evoke something in someone in our community that is healing to us. We honor them by risking being vulnerable and open to their healing energy. Our neediness allows them to serve. And so it goes.

Ultimately, what makes the part of us that feels inadequate and insecure, our scared one, feel safe? The participation of others in the journey of our lives in a meaningful, loving, and compassionate way. It's in the safety of that whole that our part feels not only safe but connected to our own wholeness and to 'Love's confusing joy.'

CHAPTER 16

PLAYFULNESS

Researchers did a study where they took a group of children, divided them into two equal, smaller groups and said, "Okay, we're going to have an art contest." To one group they said, "We're going to bring in artists to judge your creations. The best will get this prize; number two will get this prize; number three will get this prize. Here are your materials. You all go create your masterpieces and we'll bring the judges in after you're finished."

With the other group the instructions were different. "Here's all your art materials. We want you to create whatever you want. We have three prizes and we're going to do a drawing for the prizes later. What we are interested in you doing is creating whatever you want with these materials. Then we'd like to look at them when you're finished. Then, we'll do the drawing for the prizes."

They brought the artist judges in and did not tell them what paintings came from which group. And, not surprisingly, the kids who were competing for the prizes against each other, made art that was predictable. They were trying to draw something they thought would win the prize. And in so doing, they weren't creative or innovative. They defeated themselves in the process of trying to figure out what would most interest the judges and therefore be the winner.

The other kids were innovative and joyfully engaged in the creative experience. What they did was artistically much more pleasing, and the judges selected them out.

We've been talking about creativity. In organizational systems, people are interested in problem-solving. We know that if we can lighten up, be more buoyant and playful, we'll be more creative. And creativity is important in problem-solving. We know play in general is important because as animal brain size increases the amount that animals play increases. So there has to be an evolutionary advantage to play.

Often, when we're dealing with problem-solving, what we do is furrow up the brow and make it a heavy, serious thing. "We've got an issue and we need to meet immediately to deal with this issue. Cancel everything. We meet in five minutes." People come into the room, and you can feel the heaviness. It's not light and buoyant. It's heavy, serious, and stressful.

Let me tell you about a patient of mine who taught me something very important about creativity and problem-solving. Graham was a third-grader who came to see me with a brain tumor. His parents inflicted me upon him to help him deal with the stress of the cancer and treatments. When you have a brain tumor, often the first thing that happens is that you have surgery. And before surgery on your brain, you have your head shaved. Now it's hip to shave your head, but in the mid-1980s it wasn't.

Going to the hospital is a scary experience for adults. Imagine what it's like for a child. Graham goes to the hospital, gets his head shaved, and the next day gets his brain operated on. They can't get all of the tumor at surgery, so during his recovery he has the certain knowledge that there's cancer left in his brain. He goes back to his hometown to recover from his surgery and to begin his follow-up treatments. Every so often he travels two hundred miles back and forth from his hometown to Kansas City to see the specialist and to visit with me.

191

When Graham goes back to school, he looks different. His hair is gone. When we were little kids, did we hear that different was good? Was different a good thing? No. The parent says, "I don't want you playing over there with them, they're not like us. Why don't you go over and play with them, they're like us." Arthur Schopenhauer, the renowned German philosopher, said there are only a couple of things that make god laugh. One is to think we have nothing in common with someone else.

Graham goes back to school, he looks different, and he's weak from surgery. At recess, do you want to choose Graham to be on your kickball team? No. Why not? Because he's weak from surgery. He's a sure out. So Graham is chosen last.

Graham is dealing with a very heavy load. He's got cancer, he doesn't feel good, he doesn't fit in. He has a well-loaded psyche.

After surgery, Graham had to have chemotherapy and radiation treatments. After he'd completed the radiation therapy, he came to Kansas City to visit the radiation oncologist in follow-up and afterward, came to see me. When he walked in my office, he handed me a sack of noses—you know, like a pig nose, elephant nose, duck nose, shark nose—the kind of play noses you can put over your own. And he said, "Hey, doc. I've got a present for you," and handed me the sack of noses. And then he went on to say, "You know I just had my last visit with the x-ray doc. And, you know, sometimes when you go to see the doc you have to wait . . . Well I was in the room waiting for the doc to come in, and I was getting kind of bored. Then, I got this idea. I got the noses out, took the pig nose out of the sack, put it on, and waited for the doc to come to the door. When I heard him begin to turn the doorknob, I stood up and put my back to the door. When he came in and said, 'Hey Graham, How ya doin'?' I said, as I slowly turned around, 'Well doc, there are certain side-effects from the radiation you forgot to tell me about.' "

At that moment something slipped into place in my psyche, *kerchunk*. I knew I was learning something important. I thought I knew how to be with suffering people. I gave myself permission to feel their pain as much as anyone can feel the pain of another person and to be with them at their bedside, giving myself permission to express my own feelings through my tears. Graham taught me that there's another way to be with suffering people—a way that is light, buoyant, and playful.

Graham was having to deal with a life-threatening illness in his INbox, a situation that was very serious and heavy. And he managed that by finding lightness and buoyancy to maintain some kind of balance, some sense of perspective. He wasn't in denial; he was dealing with the reality of his situation and dealing with it constructively. That meets a criteria for emotional maturity. He was teaching me something about emotional maturity through playfulness.

Because of Graham I started going into the hospital and encouraging my patients to misbehave. I mean if normal isn't healthy, what's required is misbehavior. And now I do it routinely as a clown.

I have a clown character, named Dr. Jerko, who is a large-butted proctologist. On the back of his coat, it says, "I'm interested in your stools." Have you ever been in the hospital yourself. If you have, you probably recognize that in the hospital everybody's interested in your stools. For instance, the nurse comes by in the morning and says, "Did you have a bowel movement today?"

"Well, yes I did."

"Well where is it?"

"Well," pointing over to the bathroom, "I left it in there."

And the nurse goes in, looks, and says, "It's not in here."

"Well, I flushed it away."

"Well I've got to document it." (You see sometimes you've got to poop to get out.)

What would happen if that patient decided to misbehave, and even though he's sick, have a little fun? It's interesting. I've found that even people who are very sick like to laugh and have fun. "Elect yourself." Why is that? Even terminally ill people like to laugh and have fun. Why? It feels better, and THEY'RE NOT DEAD YET!

Let's say the patient decides to misbehave. The nurse comes by in the morning and says, "Did you have a bowel movement today?"

"Well yes I did," as he brings his hand out from under the covers, holding a pile of fake poop.

How would the nurse respond? First, taken aback, she might wonder, "Is that real shit?" Then she would laugh and say, "Give me that poop." And she'd go off and want to play the joke on somebody else.

What would happen to the energy on the floor? It would go up, lighten up, be healthier, driven by the sick person who's willing to break the rules.

What are we capable of if we're willing to break the rules? "It is not right to be proper," for the right reasons.

When grownups think about play, we think about competition. Grownups turn play into work. It's a zero sum game with winners and losers. The more we get away from the competitive—putting someone else down to win—game plan for life, the more fun we can have creating the movie of our lives. I think competition is important. But I think it's best when it's me competing with me. In other words, the me who's trying to be that which I'm capable of being versus the me who lives out of a conditioned database of responses.

I'm not here to compete with other people. I'm here to compete with me. I'm here to do what I can do to move on with my life developmentally, to unfold my potential in the service of others, not to put someone else down to feel better. Somebody else doesn't have to lose for me to win.

What can I do to get that part of me out of the way that needs to win? Watch myself, pay attention, let the observer effect come into play. With awareness I can go for win-win. Collaboration is about win-win. I have a small brain. You have a small brain. They are good brains but they are small. But, when you put two small but good brains together, the result is a bigger brain. The effect can be more than additive, it can be synergistic. One plus one equals three.

My attention is on doing what I do, as well as I can do it. I know that anything I do, I can do better. But, in order to get to that next level of performance, I may need to collaborate with other people. I send something to my editor. She takes what I submit and then makes it better. But, when we get together and go over the text simultaneously, what results is better than what either of us would do on our own.

People talk about the survival of the fittest and how only the strong survive. That only takes us to a certain place developmentally. What will happen to the planet if we continue to compete and see things as 'us' and 'them.' If other people have to lose for us to win, we'll eventually go from win-lose to lose-lose for *Homo sapiens*. And, only the strong will remain, the inhabitants of the microbial world will demonstrate their ability to survive on a planet inhospitable to humans. They were here before us and will be here long after we're gone. But, I see no reason to hasten to the inevitable.

So, at some point, we have to recognize the value of collaboration. We all have good brains, but they're small brains. If we put our brains together we have a bigger brain. And when we get the bigger brain working on things, creatively, it's amazing what we come up with. When we can create environments where people use their collective big brain to problem-solve, better solutions abound.

Mike Vance, author and speaker, used to be at Disney University. He talks about creativity and uses a storyboarding process for problem-solving. Everyone is given note cards and then they begin a creative planning session. He asks participants to write down their creative ideas on the cards. They are instructed not to worry about how wild their ideas sound because, the wilder the better.

He might give them a really outrageous example of a way to address a problem, to get people to free up their thinking. There is only one rule. No one is allowed to make negative comments about any of the ideas. And, all the ideas from the note cards are given equal stature as they are placed on the wall.

Then, after all the ideas are up, it is time to do the critical planning component. The critical planning session is the time to critically analyze the ideas. The result is that the creative process is separate and distinct from the critical analysis. Each idea is examined to see its merits only after all ideas are storyboarded.

Separating the creative act from the critical work allows the collective imagination to cook up solutions that might not be submitted if immediately exposed to public scrutiny. This creates a healthy environment for the fearful scared one to risk more creativity, to risk actually sharing ideas. Remember the scared one is always fearful of being exposed as inadequate. Separating the critical from the creative downsizes that risk.

Mixing the creative process and the critical analysis stifles the former. But, because normal isn't healthy, we grow up doing exactly that. In our homes, as an example, the little kid at the table says, "I had this really neat idea. I just think it would be fun if we got going real fast on the sled and went off the cliff with a parachute."

"You dummy!" the sibling says. "That's a stupid idea. You cannot go off a cliff in a sled. You would be one dead kid. You are so stupid." Ever experience this sort of sibling put down? What's interesting for the parent, in that scenario, is what it's saying about the child who needs to put their sibling down. Right then, that child is not feeling too good about himself. And if the parent doesn't understand that dynamic, he may help that child feel worse.

"You big dummy. What the hell's wrong with you. Don't call your brother stupid. How many times do I have to tell you? Maybe he's not the one who's stupid. You are . . . When you point your finger at someone else, there are three fingers pointing back at you. If there's anyone that's stupid here it must be me for thinking that you kids are ever going to shape up. You're a day late and a dollar short. The lord said 'brains,' and you thought he said 'trains' and missed every one of 'em. Stupid is as stupid does. You look stupid enough. Do you have to act stupid too? Who beat you with the stupid stick? Your stupid friends?

It burns me up to have to keep reminding you over and over and over and over. Are you listening to me? Look at me. Did you hear me?"

Lighten up, enlightenment, humm . . .

Tuesdays With Morrie is a best-selling book about a retired professor who gets ALS and is reunited with a former student, who's now a journalist. Together they chronicle his journey and life lessons through his last days. Near the end, the journalist asked Morrie if he could take a treatment that would magically restore him to his former, premorbid state, would he?

Morrie said no. He had begun to address the ultimate questions, as a result of his infirmity and for that he was grateful. He wouldn't have done so without it. When queried by his former student, Morrie said that the ultimate questions had to do with responsibility, love, spirituality, and awareness.

When I read this section of the book, I immediately thought about another retired professor, Ashley Montagu, and his definition of health: the ability to work, love, play, and think soundly. Not only did both men come up with a set of four, but a set that pretty well matched.

It was interesting for me to think about the relationship of health to the ultimate questions. How could one be healthy without confronting the ultimate questions? I don't think you can. But it was interesting to me that Morrie, who by all accounts was a vital, bright, exceptional teacher and devoted family man, had to get sick to get healthy.

That's a good example of nor . . . rather high normal not being healthy. Now, when you look at the two sets of four items, you probably see the obvious. Work and responsibility are a match. Awareness and think soundly, likewise, are a match. Love is present in each set. But play and spirituality are the lone members of their respective sets that don't seem to have a counterpart.

But, did you guess? That is another good example of why normal isn't healthy. We learn to see play and spirituality as very different things. How sad. I think it has to do with our tragic ethos.

Rumi, once more, dissolves the perceived difference.

"Speak quickly, I can't hold this one still for long.

Whoops. Don't let him kick you.

This is a wild one!" . . .

" Now get out of here,

Before this horse kicks you in the head! Easy, now!" . . .

"Back away.

I'm going to turn this rascal around!"

He gave a loud whoop and rode back,

Calling the children around him.

"One more question, Master!"

The Sheikh circled,

"What is ist? Quickly! That rider over there needs me.

I think I'm in love."

"What is this playing that you do?

Why do you hide your intelligence so?"

"The people here

want ot put me in charge. They want me to be

Judge, Magistrate, and Interpreter of all the tests.

The Knowing I have doesn't want that. It wants to enjoy itself.

I am a plantation of sugarcane, and at the same time

I'm eating the sweetness."

    Knowledge that is acquired

Is not like this. Those who have it worry if

Audiences like it or not.

      It's a bait for popularity.

Disputational knowing wants customers.

It has no soul.

    Robust and energetic

Before a responsive crowd, it slumps when no one is there.

The only real customer is God.

    Chew quietly

Your sweet sugarcane God-Love, and stay

Playfully childish.

    Your face

Will turn rosy with illumination

Like the redbud flowers.

The teacher, riding a stick horse as he plays with the children, speaks to us across the centuries. "Chew quietly your sweet sugarcane God-Love, and stay playfully childish."

Whatever else you do, will not matter. You will illuminate a sick world with your own shining face. It's so darn easy to have fun. Too bad more people don't know it.

You'll be having the time of your life, and you'll be the surprise along the way. Not only will you surprise others, but you'll surprise yourself.

Of course, if I were you, I wouldn't believe anything I say without testing it. You might want to test what we've been talking about, take what's useful, and forget the rest. I'm just like you, scratching my head and trying to figure out what the heck is going on. Don't forget I have that big sign on my office door:

"Caution.

Beware of Doc.

Enter at your own risk.

I make mistakes every day."

About the Author

[to come]

Hazelden Information and Educational Services is a division of the Hazelden Foundation, a not-for-profit organization. Since 1949, Hazelden has been a leader in promoting the dignity and treatment of people afflicted with the disease of chemical dependency.

The mission of the foundation is to improve the quality of life for individuals, families, and communities by providing a national continuum of information, education, and recovery services that are widely accessible; to advance the field through research and training; and to improve our quality and effectiveness through continuous improvement and innovation.

Stemming from that, the mission of this division is to provide quality information and support to people wherever they may be in their personal journey—from education and early intervention, through treatment and recovery, to personal and spiritual growth.

Although our treatment programs do not necessarily use everything Hazelden publishes, our bibliotherapeutic materials support our mission and the Twelve Step philosophy upon which it is based. We encourage your comments and feedback.

The headquarters of the Hazelden Foundation is in Center City, Minnesota. Additional treatment facilities are located in Chicago, Illinois; New York, New York; Plymouth, Minnesota; St. Paul, Minnesota; and West Palm Beach, Florida. At these sites, we provide a continuum of care for men and women of all ages. Our Plymouth facility is designed specifically for youth and families.

For more information on Hazelden, please call **1-800-257-7800**. Or you may access our World Wide Web site on the Internet at **www.hazelden.org.**